SAP EDI, IDOC, and Interfacing Interview Questions, Answers, and Explanations

---

SAPCOOKBOOK.COM

Please visit our website at www.sapcookbook.com
© 2006 Equity Press all rights reserved.

ISBN 1-933804-07-6

The programs in this book have been included for instructional value only. They have been tested with care but are not guaranteed for any particular purpose. The publisher does not offer any warranties or representations not does it accept any liabilities with respect to the programs.

Trademark notices

SAP, SAP EBP, SAP SRM, Netweaver, and SAP New Dimension are registered trademarks of SAP AG. This publisher gratefully acknowledges SAP permission to use its trademark in this publication. SAP AG is not the publisher of this book and is not responsible for it under any aspect of the law.

TABLE OF CONTENTS

- v -

SAP EDI, IDOC, and Interfacing Interview Questions, Answers, and Explanations

By Jim Stewart

SAPCOOKBOOK
Equity Press

☞ QUESTION 1

Output File With Filled Inbound IDOC File

Is it possible to create an output file with a filled inbound IDOC file for the purpose of creating an inbound DESADV shipping notification?

✍ ANSWER

You could "test" using transaction code WE19. Construct your own IDOC file with this tool, fill the fields of the segments (control + data) and submit. Generally, the obligatory fields of the IDOC file segments are the same as the fields in the online transaction.

☞ **QUESTION 2**

Flat File Creation

How can I create a flat file from IDOC file generated through transaction code WE19 for outbound processing?

✍ **ANSWER**

Choose the standard outbound processing and send the created IDOC file to your file. Port type file is maintained in transaction codes WE20 and WE21.

☞ QUESTION **3**

Single Partner Profile

We have approximately 100 different customers we want to send EDI invoices to. The Business Connector will treat each customer in the same way with the same XML schema sent to the same URL. Can a group of customers be setup as a single partner profile in transaction code WE20, or will we need to set up a partner profile for each one?

✍ ANSWER

First create a customer profile. Then create a partner profile for this group of customers. Include a partner ID in the partner function RE -Bill to Party on each of the sold-to which you want to combine.

☞ **QUESTION 4**

How To Handle Change Pointers For Table ADR6 For DEBMAS

I need change pointers activation for table ADR6 for message type DEBMAS. However, the standard function module 'MASTERIDOC_CREATE_SMD_DEBMAS' is not reading change pointers for table ADR6 (object ADRESSE). What must I do to obtain change pointers activation for table ADR6?

✐ **ANSWER**

In order to obtain change pointers activation implement transaction code BD52.

☞ QUESTION 5

Populate Extended IDOC File Segments

How do you populate extended IDOC file segments?

✍ ANSWER

Once you extend an IDOC file, it is an enhancement of the standard IDOC file. Write some coding in the USER-EXIT for each outbound/inbound message. Go to CMOD and search for whether the message type exists for the user exit. If the message type exists take that exit in the CMOD, and create a project and write the code.

☞ QUESTION 6

RFC SAP -> Excel Via VB -> More Parameters

I am attempting to extract stocks from SAP/R3 to Excel via VB using the code in Figure 1. When I run the code, I receive the stock for material 123 on plant 0001 and storage location 0001 (See figure 2). Then I receive the error message "System Failure". The code works fine for one parameter, but I need to extract the material, the plant and the storage location. Is it possible to do this?

Figure 1 (abridged)
```
'connect to SAP
'call function
Set MyFunc = R3.Add("RFC_READ_TABLE")

Set oParam1 = MyFunc.Exports("QUERY_TABLE")
Set oParam2 = MyFunc.Tables("FIELDS")
Set oParam3 = MyFunc.Tables("OPTIONS")
Set oParam4 = MyFunc.Exports("DELIMITER")
```

Figure 2 (abridged)
```
' materials to select, please choose from your number range
oParam3.Rows.Add
oParam3.Value(1, "TEXT") = "MATNR = 000000000000000123"
oParam3.Rows.Add
oParam3.Value(2, "TEXT") = "WERKS = 0001"
oParam3.Rows.Add
oParam3.Value(3, "TEXT") = "LGORT = 0001"
```

✍ ANSWER

The select code in the RFC looks like this: select * from (query_table) into work where (options). The options must look like a "where" clause, but without the "where". Instead, put "and" in front of the second and third lines of the code in Figure 2.

☞ QUESTION 7

SAP Gateway Failure

I have been using a simple program that would access some information in the R3 system. However, each time I run the code, I receive an error. Must I configure something on the portal and/or the SAP R/3 system? Does SAProuters have something to do with these parameters?

✍ ANSWER

If there is a SAP router, you must include it. The simplest way to do this is to add it to the beginning of the server address/name, surrounded by /H/ (upper case is important). Also, check your services file for the SAPgw00 entry to make sure the system knows which port to connect to.

☞ QUESTION 8

Creating Inbound Delivery Via DESADV

What are the required fields and/or segments for Message Type DESADV? I am attempting to create an inbound delivery via the test tool transaction code WE19.

✍ ANSWER

Here is an example of a working IDOC file:

```
E1EDL20 LIFEX=testASN
E1EDT13 QUALF=007 NTANF=20051215
E1EDL24 POSNR=00001 KDMAT=ABCD LFIMG=24.000
VRKME=PCE
E1EDL41 QUALI=001 BSTNR=4500056164
POSEX=00001
```

Be sure to include some shipment details in your IDOC file, such as the following:

```
E1EDL37-EXIDV
E1EDL37-VHILM_KU
E1EDL44-EXIDV
```

☞ QUESTION 9

Qualifiers and Message Types

Where can I find documentation on what each qualifier is and what is mandatory for message types in general?

✍ ANSWER

View the User Settings on transaction code WE60.

☞ QUESTION 10

RSRLDREL Program Function

While inserting values into table SRRELROLES, I found an OSS note and it suggested running program RSRLDREL. What is the purpose of this report and what type of IDOC files will it delete?

✍ ANSWER

This program deletes relations and roles from the database for which no instance of objects exist in the Business Object Repository (BOR). The existence of objects is only checked for the local system. It also deletes the links between IDOC files and application documents if one of the documents has been archived. For example, if your company archives IDOC files you can run this program to have the IDOC file number link removed from the application documents that they posted.

☞ **QUESTION 11**

Business Connector Flat File Record Terminated

I must create a flat file in Business Connector. Each record is terminated with hex 0A (Line feed). I want to do this by inserting the value at the end of the string. How do I type this into the set value field of the built in service I am using?

✍ **ANSWER**

Enter the line feed in a text editor (e.g. Ultra Edit) and afterwards copy this single value from there by placing STRG+C into the set value box with STRG+V. After processing the service you could do another test by copying the processed flat file into the text editor again and check the result.

☞ QUESTION 12

Parsing IDOC Files

I am looking for tools to parse IDOC files, preferably in PERL. Would converting to XML be the best decision?

✍ ANSWER

It is easy to parse IDOC files in Java if you receive them by RFC with JCO and its IDOC file option. If your needs are simple, you may develop your own parser. If you need to parse files to convert them, use some market tool. AnyTrans is an effective tool.

☞ QUESTION 13

Filter Group Creation

When I am creating my distribution model and adding my Z message I do not have the option to add filter groups. How do I create a filter group for my message?

✍ ANSWER

To create a filter group, implement transaction codes BD59 and BD95.

☞ QUESTION **14**

Fast Interface Between SAP And External System

I am conducting regular transfers of 70000 documents between an external system and SAP. It seems that batch input (transaction code SM35) is not suitable in this case, since performance is essential. What is the best technology for importing large amounts of data in SAP?

✍ ANSWER

Use IDOC files or a BAPI. Batch input was the best way to do this in the past, but there are better methods now.

☞ **QUESTION 15**

PO Output Through EDI

Currently we are printing purchase orders with two methods. One is using PRINTER and another is using EDI Output. I modified the custom SAP script and the output from PRINTER is working fine. However, when a purchase order is created with NB, the EDI output is triggered automatically and creates an IDOC file. What is the problem?

✍ **ANSWER**

Check your conditions and access sequences at: Menu Path - Logistics/Materials Management/Purchasing/Messages. This is where you control the output for a message type.

☞ QUESTION **16**

Vehicle IDOC File To SAP System

I am using Seebeyond as middleware and sending a vehicle IDOC file to VEHCLE01 to SAP System. Should I use an Application Link Enabling or EDI scenario partner type?

✍ ANSWER

Use an EDI scenario for this situation.

☞ QUESTION 17

Inserting New Lines Using PO Change IDOC File

I am attempting to use purchases order change IDOC file PORDCH01 to insert a new line item into the purchase order. Is this possible?

✍ ANSWER

To insert new lines using the purchase interface, check the PO_ITEMX flag in the E1BPMEPOITEMX segment.

☞ QUESTION 18

IDOC File Inbound Function

We have a PC that triggers an IDOC file through MQSeries. The IDOC file is then generated in SAP which calls a function which prints a Packing Slip. The above function was slightly modified and now works in Development/Test, as well as, in Production when in debug. But when executed in Production by the PC (background), the function acts like the old version. What is wrong?

✍ ANSWER

Make sure the generated function is correctly transported.

☞ QUESTION **19**

Filename For IDOC Files

Where are the IDOC files stored on the SAP system before being passed on to the EDI subsystem? What is the filename and location?

✍ ANSWER

The filename and locations are, in order, EDIDC and EDID4.

☞ **QUESTION 20**

Searching Within IDOC Files

If an IDOC file fails because data within the IDOC file is not correct, is there a fast way to search for error lines within the IDOC file?

✍ **ANSWER**

Table EDID4 includes all the header and segment data of an IDOC file. Use transaction code SE16 to data browse the table. Another alternative is to implement transaction code WE09. It retrieves IDOC files that match the condition you input (e.g. segment, field and value.).

☞ QUESTION 21

Determining VAT Code

Within our company we want to move to EDI invoicing. How do I determine the correct VAT code based on the VAT rates on the incoming EDI invoices?

✍ ANSWER

The entries you may specify in trans OBCD are not detailed enough to correctly process invoices. To resolve this issue, specify not the tax-rate but another more specific value in OBCD (such as the supplier number).

Use a user exit to replace the incoming VAT-rate in the IDOC file to this more specific value (in this case the supplier number).

☞ **QUESTION 22**

IDOC File Orders Documentation With Qualifier List

I need to perform a mapping with two different structures. I use the standard IDOC file ORDERS (orders05). While the fields are automatically filled by the system, I do not know exactly where the data is in the IDOC file and I do not exactly know the qualifier that is used by the system.

✍ **ANSWER**

In transaction code WE60, go to the menu Go to -> User Settings. Check the options for Documentation Output and Field Value Output. Now, if you run the transaction again, you should receive the qualifiers as well.

☞ **QUESTION 23**

EDI_DC Control Record IDOC File In 3.1h

It appears that the EDI_DC control record of any IDOC file from 4.6 is different from that in 3.1h. Looking at the record purely as a flat file, the data is in different positions. How do you make a 4.6 IDOC file into a 3.1h IDOC file style?

✍ **ANSWER**

If you want to have an IDOC file in 3.0/3.1 format. You should configure this in the transaction code WE21 in the PORT definition.

☞ QUESTION 24

Mapping E1edka1

I am having trouble with SAP mapping the field E1EDKA1 into the IDOC file ORDERS05 through function module IDOC_output_orders. How do I do this?

✍ ANSWER

E1EDKA1 is a segment, not a field in an IDOC file. If you check subroutine fuellen_IDOC_inttab in function module IDOC_output_orders, E1EDKA1 is mapped.

☞ QUESTION 25

Change Pointers From Custom IDOC File

I have created a custom IDOC file for Z-Table in which the particular field has the change document enabled. I have created this particular entry in transaction code BD52. Where is it creating the entry in CDHDR since it is not creating an entry in transaction codes BDCPS or BDCP? How may I enable a change pointers entry for a custom IDOC file so that I trigger an IDOC file?

✍ ANSWER

Use transaction code BD21 for change pointers and transaction code BD22 to delete change pointers.

☞ QUESTION 26

File Port

I have created a file port and I have given it the path /interface/
country/file. We have a program that creates the file using a
function module that creates the file name. Other non-SAP
servers give us an FTP address, login and password within
a folder. When we ran the program it created the IDOC files
on specific file ports. When we ran Rseout00 it collected the
IDOC files and sent them to our path interface/country/file,
which I define in file port. After that must I manually FTP the
file? Is this process correct and is the file port meant to work
in this manner?

✍ ANSWER

Create a file port and write an FTP script that automatically
transfers the file. You only need to specify the file port with
the function.

☞ **QUESTION 27**

How To Set IDOC File Status Using ABAP Routine

I have an ABAP program that reads several IDOC files with status 3 (port OK). After processing them I must change the status to 6 (translation OK). Is there a function module or routine in ABAP that does this or if I should modify it directly in table EDIDC?

✍ **ANSWER**

You should use the following function modules to change an IDOC file status: EDI_DOCUMENT_STATUS_SET , IDOC_STATUS_WRITE_TO_DATABASE.

☞ QUESTION **28**

Application Link Enabling (ALE) Interface Definition

What is an Application Link Enabling interface?

✍ ANSWER

ALE or Application Link Enabling is the technical basis for integrating business processes in a distributed system environment. It includes developer and testing tools and preconfigured Application Link Enabling Business Processes delivered in the standard R/3 Release. Application Link Enabling has functions for managing messaging and for handling communication and application errors.

☞ QUESTION 29

Determining IDOC File Source

Is it possible to determine if the source of an IDOC file is Application Link Enabling or EDI?

✍ ANSWER

Yes, if the IDOC file Control is Logical System, then the IDOC file is from Application Link Enabling. Otherwise, it is EDI.

☞ **QUESTION 30**

BAPI/RFC For Maintaining Components

In a 4.6b environment, is there a BAPI or RFC for maintaining components in a BOM?

✍ **ANSWER**

You should maintain components in BOM using the following RFC function module: CSAP_MAT_BOM_MAINTAIN.

☞ **QUESTION 31**

Processing An IDOC File Through Transaction Code BD87

When I attempt to process an IDOC file through transaction code BD87, I receive the following error: 'No batch data input for screen'. Application document not posted. What am I doing wrong?

✍ **ANSWER**

Some of the SAP standard function modules for processing IDOC files internally use BDCs. The problem is with the BDC and it could be either missing data for the screen or it could also be a pop-up message. Analyze the screen fields. You could also reprocess this IDOC file via transaction code WE19 instead of transaction code BD87. In transaction code WE19 you should tell the system to process the IDOC file in foreground and this should bring up the BDC screen.

☞ QUESTION **32**

Fast Testing Of A RFC Connection Destination

I am having trouble with the following function:

CALL FUNCTION 'RFC_PING' DESTINATION DEST
TABLES RFCTAB40 = RFCTAB
EXCEPTIONS SYSTEM_FAILURE = 1
MESSAGE RFC_MESS
COMMUNICATION_FAILURE = 2
MESSAGE RFC_MESS.

It is from SAP and it runs into the routine to "test" a TCP/IP Destination connection. (See SM59). When you execute it the connection has problems. Before the function issues the exception COMMUNICATIONS_FAILURE, there is a wait time that lasts several seconds: Do you know a function module or procedure to quickly check if the connection has problems, avoiding any wait time?

✍ ANSWER

If your RFC destination is specified by a hostname, make it an IP address to eliminate the time for hostname>IP address resolution. It is not SAP but a ping at OS level that tries many times to send packets and it takes time. You could also 'ping' with options like -n (Number of echo request to send) or -w (Timeout in milliseconds to wait for each reply). Options may differ depending on the platform. It should be done like this: Create 'ping' command at OS level. Call the command against the destination you want to check with option parameters -n and/or -w. Check returned message from 'ping' and make sure it was delivered.

☞ QUESTION **33**

Calling R3 Functions From XI

Is it possible to call R3 RFC functions from XI without ABAP?

✍ ANSWER

Yes. You must import the BAPI into XI under imported Objects, RFCs. You should import IDOC files in a similar way under imported Objects, IDOC files. Map the fields from sender to receiver or vice versa and the postings will be made as long as the commit transaction function module is added to the BAPI.

☞ QUESTION 34

Post Goods Issued Date

I am using DELVRY03 and I must post goods issued. However, I cannot find any field in the IDOC file for the post goods issued date. Is there a field in the IDOC file for this date?

✍ ANSWER

You should find the post goods issued date in E1EDT13-NTANF field (qualifier QUALF= '006').

☞ QUESTION **35**

URL For Open Document Method

I am attempting to open a word document saved on my front end, on a control area on a SAP window, but I do not know how to build the corresponding URL. What should I do?

✍ ANSWER

In order to open the document, build the URL this way: file://c:/temp/test.doc.

☞ **QUESTION 36**

SDPACK Inbound IDOC File

The same IDOC file runs in background and dialogue depending on the sender. We are having a problem with the SDPACK inbound IDOC file. It was working fine sending from our datapass server to SAP 4.6. We added another datapass server and now this new server does not work properly. The IDOC file processes correctly (document is packed) but output determination is not run for the delivery. I have processed the same IDOC file contents through both servers and they both behave differently when processing. I ran a trace on both and each go through different programs, but both are SDPACK IDOC files. What could be causing the problem?

✍ **ANSWER**

The new server is likely running an older version of SAPGUI and must be upgraded. The SAPGUI must be accessed from the server when running IDOC files.

☞ **QUESTION 37**

Message Type MATERIAL CODE

We want to send material data to multiple logical systems. At the sender level the material should be created in several plants. We want to use plant as a filter group. Material created in plant 1, would be sent to logical system 1. Material created in plant 2, would be sent to logical system 2. How should we configure this?

✍ **ANSWER**

You should define two model views for message type MATERIAL CODE, and assign the plant code into each model view.

☞ QUESTION 38

Error In Distribution Model

When I am distributing a model in transaction code BD64 I am receiving the following message: "Model view ZALEKFINO2 has not been updated."

The maintenance system for model view ZALEKFINO2 is sending to a system in the US, but the maintenance system in receiving is in Germany. Should I delete the model on the receiving side and then distribute it from the sending side?

✍ ANSWER

Yes, you must delete the model on the receiving side then re-distribute it. If there are different distribution models already defined for the same combination of logical systems on the receiving system, you receive this message.

☞ QUESTION **39**

Time Involved In Setting Up A SAP Business Connector

My customer is running a 4.6C system. He asked me for a rough estimate on the time involved in setting up a SAP Business Connector with one standard interface to one distributor. Business Connector should only convert IDOC file to XML without any additional mappings. I know that the installation is very simple. How much time is involved in implementing this single interface?

✍ ANSWER

If there is no mapping involved and you communicate with SAP-XML, a rough estimate of the time involved (regardless of the OS) would be: OS installed and an anti-virus. Installation by one SAP Business Connector: 30 minutes to one hour. Patching of one SAP Business Connector: 1 hour . Additional setup: 1 hour Integration with SAP: 4 hours (including SAP system setup). Message setup: 4 hours (over-estimated). Reverse invoke setup: 2 hours. Connection with partner: 1 hour. Test of sending/receiving with partner: one week at least.

☞ QUESTION **40**

IDOC File Error During Application

I tried the IDOC file in transaction code BD87 in foreground but I am receiving the error message: Error during application process. What is the problem?

✍ ANSWER

Before reprocessing the IDOC file, you must analyze the message of the application error to suppress the cause. You should receive the detailed message from transaction code BD87 by double-clicking on the status 51. For example, you may have an error because you are attempting to post on a closed financial period. You must open the period before attempting to process again (or create an IDOC file with a different date if your business process does not allow posting in the past.)

☞ QUESTION 41

IDOC File Status History

How do you view the IDOC file status history?

✍ ANSWER

Select the IDOC file with transaction code WE02. Double click on the IDOC file you wish to display. On the left side, you will have both the IDOC file content (segments) and the status history (successive status values). By clicking on the status, you will receive even more details, such as time and user ID.

☞ QUESTION 42

Uploading Data Using LSMW

I have used IDOC file of LSMW to upload Characteristics master, the Message Type should be: CHRMAS and Basic Type should be: CHRMAS01, but I face a problem when I execute the step "Start IDOC file Generation." The system shows the error "No partner exists with the name", type." What data is missing?

✍ ANSWER

When you are using a BAPI or an IDOC file for uploading data using LSMW, you need to configure the port and the partner type for the LSMW object before uploading the data. You should do that in the initial screen of LSMW transaction.

LSMW -> Settings -> IDOC file Inbound Processing.

☞ **QUESTION 43**

Create An IDOC File When Vendor Is Updated

I am attempting to create integration where an IDOC file is sent each time a vendor is updated. Today we are using a job that calls the program RBDSECRE to send an IDOC file of updated vendor. The problem is that it sends all updated vendors every time. Is there a user exit for calling the program when a vendor is updated?

✍ **ANSWER**

You should implement EXIT_SAPMF02K_001 function module (user exit) with include name MF02KFEX.

☞ QUESTION 44

Invoice Credit Error

I am attempting to bring in a vendor invoice but I am receiving an error: "Balance not zero: 2,030.00- debits: 2,030.00 credits: 0.00". The invoice amount is 2,030. I am using INVOIC01, message type INVOIC, process code INVL. Should I add an offsetting entry for the credit?

✍ ANSWER

Use absolute values. Your debit/credit indicator already takes care of the sign. Also ensure Credit = Debit

☞ **QUESTION 45**

User Exit For Outbound GLMAST

I am attempting to send the outbound IDOC file of GL Master (glmast01) where I would like to add a few fields that are not part of the standard IDOC file. What is the user exit for the outbound IDOC file?

✍ **ANSWER**

There is no user exit for outbound GLMAST. Instead of using user exit, you might want to create your own function module that wraps outbound GLMAST module.

☞ QUESTION 46

Creating A New Partner Type LS

When I want to create a new Partner Type LS, I was asked to enter a "partner number". Where should I define this partner number? When I tried to input something, the prompt stated "'Enter a permissible partner number".

✍ ANSWER

You must define logical systems.

Transaction code SALE > Sending and Receiving Systems > Logical Systems > Define Logical System

☞ **QUESTION 47**

Incompletion Log To ORDRSP

Is there an easy way to pass on the incompletion log of a sales order to the order response IDOC file? If the price on EDI (incoming IDOC file) does not match the system price, the system flags the order as incomplete. We want to send this information to the customer in the order response IDOC file. Is this possible?

✍ **ANSWER**

Yes. You must configure Message control outbound for this message type and when it is saved, this message, ordrsp, will be sent automatically to external system. You need to indicate this in partner profile for outbound.Once you send this message, you need to use a user exit to "catch" the message content, read the incompletion log and put the text found inside the message in an empty field of the message or in an extended segment of the ordrsp.

☞ **QUESTION 48**

Finding A Program That Triggers IDOC File

I am searching for a program that is written to trigger IDOC file Material Code. Where would I find this?

✍ **ANSWER**

Check the function called IDOC_input_Material Code01.

☞ QUESTION 49

Changing The IDOC File Contents At The Receiving End

Is it possible to change the IDOC file contents at the receiving end?

✍ ANSWER

Use exit: ALE00001. This exit is for IDOC file version change. It will be triggered if the version of the IDOC file type or Extension for message type is different from the standard definition. In the include LBD11F11, you may select which condition the exit is triggered.

If this does not work, I would suggest that you prepare a special function module and tie it to partners by customized process code.

☞ QUESTION 50

Transfer IDOC File From SAP To External System

We have IDOC files that are saved in the SAP Application server. We are manually transferring these files to our external system. Can this be performed automatically?

✍ ANSWER

The "classic" way to do this is to obtain the files by FTP or through a Windows shared folder. If the external system will support it, you should send the IDOC file by RFC.

☞ QUESTION 51

RFC From External System To R/3

I was asked to develop a RFC that a system in AS400 will use to modify a table in R/3. How should I do this?

✍ ANSWER

Do not change any tables in SAP from outside. Use RFC functions provided by SAP or create BDC from transaction. This will help you to use SAP controls.

☞ QUESTION 52

Material BAPI Problem

I am using BAPI_MATERIAL_SAVEDATA for the material creation. I am able to create a material with all views.

I am not able to create the Product Version for the material that is at MRP View. How would I populate the data for the respective fields to update into material master?

✍ ANSWER

Unfortunately, you cannot update Product Version through BAPI_MATERIAL_SAVEDATA. Because its core program MATERIAL_MAINTAIN_DARK does not support update for MKAL, if you need to update MKAL, you may need to call MKAL_SAVE_NEW or some other function module.

☞ **QUESTION 53**

Error In Inbound IDOC File

If there is an error in inbound IDOC file, can SAP send out email?

✍ **ANSWER**

It is possible to still send email by using workflow event inputErrorOccurred. For basic configuration of this event, you should refer to SAP Help - Application Link Enabling Programming Guide - Error Handling. You may need to add an e-mail distribution step by yourself.

☞ QUESTION 54

IDOC File Reporting

I have been asked to write a report that extracts the IDOC files for that day along with their status (success or failure) and some key information stored in the segment of the IDOC file. But I cannot find the database tables that stores the segment info, i.e. reference and text fields.

I have found the EDIDC and EDIDS tables so I can output the IDOC file number, along with the system success message. I am looking for the IDOC files segment data, in particular the below fields which can view in transaction code WE02 when drilling down into the contents of the individual segments of the IDOC file. The EDIDC and EDIDS tables only contain what I call header data. Does anyone know where the segment data is stored?

✍ ANSWER

The data for the segment is stored in EDID4-SDATA. You need to create a work area for the segment you are looking at and then move SDATA into this field. This will break the SDATA segment into the fields you want to reference.

☞ **QUESTION 55**

Transaction Code WE20 Status 56 Partner Profile Not Found

Is it possible to automatically create EDI partner profiles transaction code WE20 for all customers? In my case, it is just inbound sales orders and SDPICK. Can I write a BDC session for creating transaction code WE20 for all SAP customers? The problem I encountered is that the IDOC file coming in for orders or SDPICK failed. I want to automatically create transaction code WE20 partner profiles.

✍ **ANSWER**

Implement transaction code BD82, generate partner profile.

☞ **QUESTION 56**

RFC Enabling With Java

Is it possible to RFC enable any SAP function module from Java, using the JCO or any other connector?

✍ **ANSWER**

Yes, you have the ability to call any RFC enabled function from Java with JCO.

☞ **QUESTION 57**

Running SAP Report From Java

Can we run a SAP report/transaction from Java?

✍ **ANSWER**

Yes, you may implement this report by using RFC_CALL_ FUNCTION.

☞ QUESTION 58

How To See The Backend Program For A Message Type

How can I view the backend program for any message type?

✍ ANSWER

Message types are not associated with a program. The process code is typically where you see the program. For example inbound purchase orders typically use the process code ORDE which is tied to the function module IDOC_INPUT_ ORDERS. To see the process codes go to transaction code WE41 for outbound and transaction code WE42 for inbound. Double click on any of them and you will see the processing function module. There are other means of processing but this is the most common.

☞ **QUESTION 59**

IDOC File Status Conversion

I have a problem with HR Payroll and FI/CO interface. I have an IDOC file in status 64 that is not receiving posted date nor is an application document created. Normally IDOC file converts to status 62 and then 53 automatically. Where am I going wrong?

✐ **ANSWER**

Status 64 means that IDOC file is waiting to be processed yet. Usually it occurs on a busy system when there are no free resources available at the time the IDOC file arrives. Looks like your system is not configured to process these IDOC files automatically when system recourses are available. Ask your BASIS to implement a SAP note dealing with the issue. Meanwhile, you may re-process IDOC files manually via transaction code BD87 (select node/message with status 64 and click 'Process' button).

☞ QUESTION 60

Deletion Of IDOC Files

The business has decided that it no longer needs the Application Link Enabling Sales Order IDOC files that were not transferred. As a result we are attempting to delete these historical documents (status 03). I know that we should be using the proper archiving process (via SARA) but we have not enabled archiving. I also know that I can delete IDOC files via transaction code SM58, but I have not always received authorization as the owner of the IDOC file is the owner of the SAP process that created the IDOC file. Also this is not a method of mass deleting. Does anyone know another method for mass deleting IDOC files regardless of whether they have or have not been processed?

✍ ANSWER

Implement the function module EDI_DOCUMENT_DELETE. It will delete the IDOC file. However, it only works with a single IDOC file, so you should write an ABAP for mass deletion.

☞ QUESTION 61

Partner Profile Not Maintained

We are performing the JIT Scenario where requirements are posted in SAP Scheduling Agreement 'LZ' with an Incoming IDOC file.

The incoming IDOC file currently does not identify the Control record and goes into error 56 with message "Partner Profile not available".

We have maintained the Partner profile in full. What could be the possible reason for the IDOC file behaving in such a manner?

✐ ANSWER

Double check your partner profile versus your IDOC file control record. To do this, go to transaction code SE16 and look at table EDP21 which is your inbound partner profile and EDIDC for the IDOC file control record. The fields MANDT, SNDPRN, SNDPRT, SNDPFC, MESTYP, MESCOD, MESFCT, and TEST in EDP21 must match the corresponding fields in EDIDC.

☞ QUESTION 62

Native SQL DB Links To R3

From remote Oracle databases, does anybody use Oracle DB links to the R/3 database to select R/3 transparent table data using Oracle SQL?

✍ ANSWER

Yes, but I suggest using the separate Oracle user which has rights on separate SAP transparent tables.

☞ QUESTION 63

Can Change Pointers Trigger IDOC File During Create

We have activated Change Pointers for Message type CREMAS (Vendors). I have selected half a dozen fields using transaction code BD52 that I want an IDOC file to be created for. However I also want to be able to create the IDOC file in a similar way when the Vendor is first created instead of only in change mode?

✍ ANSWER

In transaction code BD52 I had selected 11 entries for CREMAS and removed the rest. None of the entries had the values for create (which I understand are) Object Table Name Field Name: KRED LFA1 KEY

☞ QUESTION **64**

Connecting SAP to A Warehouse System

In your opinion/experience what is the best method/tool to connect R/3 to an external warehouse system? I am using a 4.5B release.

✍ ANSWER

I suggest using Radio frequency Tech.

☞ **QUESTION 65**

EDI ORDERS: Duplicate Orders Submitted/ Created

We are having a situation where we have Purchase orders coming in via EDI from our customers. We retrieve these orders every hour and process them directly into SAP. What has happened in several cases is that the customer sent duplicate POs by mistake and when the orders are created in SAP, since they are being processed at the same time, results in the same PO created twice. Does anyone have any recommendations on how to deal with this?

✍ **ANSWER**

Check the VBKD table and in the event there is a duplicate purchase order, send them to workflow.

☞ QUESTION 66

ORDERS05 For Sales Order

I am just wondering if it is possible to populate the E1EDL37/ E1EDL44 segments of the IDOC file ORDERS05 with ORDRSP when I save the sales order (rush order)?

✍ ANSWER

The standard SAP function module (idoc_output_ordrsp) does not populate those two segments, but you could insert code into the user exit EXIT_SAPLVEDC_002 to populate those segments.

☞ **QUESTION 67**

JCO Runtime Error

I am attempting to connect in R/3 using a JCO package. But when I attempt to connect I receive the following coding error: "java.lang.UnsatisfiedLinkError: no jRFC12 in java. library.path".

✍ **ANSWER**

The Java path names have not been set up correctly or perhaps the install was not correct. The JCO install guide is not quite correct. You will have success if you implement the following:

JCO install is an unpack of the latest version (SAPJCO-ntintel-x.x.x.zip) into Webserver drive C:\Jco.

Once this is unpacked the librfc32.dll and sapjcorfc.dll need to be copied from the C:\Jco into C:\WINNT\System32.

Then add via Control Panel > System > Environment vars PATH = append the C:\Jco CLASSPATH = C:\Jco\sapjco.jar.

You should also include the jRFC11.dll and jRFC12.dll in the System32 directory. If they already exist, you may need to overwrite them.

☞ **QUESTION 68**

Methodology For Extraction Of Application Data From SAP

I have an Intel-based solution to build RosettaNet based messages. And there is an existing SAP system that is churning out Purchase Orders. Is there a mechanism available in SAP which would allow me to extract the purchase order-related data in any format, and then use that date to send as a RosettaNet Message?

✍ **ANSWER**

You could set up Application Link Enabling to create an "order" IDOC file for every purchase order created. Unfortunately, it is not a simple process, especially, as this requires "message control" setup.

☞ QUESTION 69

Problem In Posting Data Into Sap R/3 From VB Using RFCS

I am using the following business flow: 1) In Visual Basic, user enters data, 2) The data posts to SAP R/3 and 3) The posted data goes into a custom table in SAP R/3. The SAP program creates a data dictionary table and a function module is created, which is remote-enabled and that posts the data supplied to it into the custom table. In Visual Basic the data will be entered in Flexi Grid by looping the contents of MSFLEXGRID. Then, the data must be supplied to the function module table. Now I am able to loop the data in MS FLEX GRID, but I am unable to populate the function module table from Visual Basic. How do I populate the function module table fields with data from the Visual Basic side when I am using RFCs to connect to SAP R/3?

✐ ANSWER

You can populate the function module table by populating the TABLE of the RFC.

Here is a code sample:

Loop thru the FLEX GRID

```
------------------------
i = i + 1
iTab.Rows.Add

iTab.Value(i, "MATNR") = (FLEXGRID value of MATNR)
iTab.Value(i, "MTART") = (FLEXGRID value of MTART)
----------------------
END Loop
```

☞ QUESTION 70

Business Connector and 4.7

We are on 4.6 and considering using Business Connector to send XML documents for the purchasing process (POs, scheduling agreements, receive inbound shipping notifications and invoices). We use standard IDOC files, and send them to the Business Connector, which formats them as XML (after some mapping), and routes them to the vendor. For the reverse process, the vendor sends an ASN or invoice to the Business Connector in XML, it maps to an IDOC file, and posts it in R/3. When we finally upgrade to 4.7, will SAP continue to support Business Connector or will we be forced to go to XI? How difficult will it be to migrate from Business Connector to XI?

✍ ANSWER

The scenario you mentioned with Business Connector is correct. That is the normal way you will do that using Business Connector .

There is no need to switch to XI just because you are upgrading your SAP system. Business Connector will do the job with 4.7 as well. However Business Connector is set to "end of life" meaning that there will be no support after the end of 2005. Nevertheless, you could then switch to WebMethods Integration Server, which is basically the same as Business Connector but sold by webMethods and not by SAP.

☞ QUESTION 71

Problem With Direct Input

I am attempting to insert a new purchase order into the R/3 through LSMW, using the DI 'rm06eeio'. The insert failed with the following errors:

"Company code of PO not match up with that of purchasing organization"
"No currency assigned to vendor"
"Item category 0 not allowed"
"Missing authorization create plant 0001"

I have succeeded in inserting the same purchase order with a BAPI, so it cannot be a customization problem. What is the coding error?

✍ ANSWER

I would say that the BAPI takes a lot more liberties in defaulting information that the direct input program does. In direct input, you need to make sure you fill in as many field as you can with the correct values.

For example, if a material is only set up in one plant, the BAPI might default this value into the PO, whereas the direct input program will not.

☞ **QUESTION 72**

IDOC_INPUT_ORDERS In 4.6B

Can someone explain why IDOC_INPUT_ORDERS in 4.6B cannot handle the creation of texts? There is a form TEXT_ CREATE which has the routines to create the header and item texts (from XE1EDKT2 and XE1EDPT2 tables) but it is not performed anywhere in the program. In older versions (e.g., 4.0B), this is handled after successful CALL TRANSACTION VA01X processing using entries in BDCDATA.

✎ **ANSWER**

Creation of text is accounted for in 4.6B. 4.6B exports the tables XE1EDKT1 and E1EDKT2 to memory and data is imported by the VA01 transaction at the appropriate time. Check in the IDOC_INPUT_ORDERS function for the line PERFORM check_text.

This is where the texts are exported. It probably does not fill the BDCDATA table with the texts anymore because the new GUI control for the text box is not call transaction friendly. Instead VA01 was modified to import any exported texts.

☞ QUESTION 73

Difference Between SAP XI And SAP Business Connector

What is the difference between SAP XI and SAP Business Connector and in what situations would I use one or the other?

✑ ANSWER

SAP XI and SAP Business Connector use completely different architectures to achieve integration between different systems. XI is used as a Central Integration Server and is aimed to minimize direct connections between different systems (all systems are connected to XI; XI routes the messages between the systems). On the other hand, Business Connector is just a translator between different systems.

You may use XI for all SAP versions starting with 3.1i. But XI itself runs on a dedicated WAS. The difference between Business Connector and XI is the Integration architecture you build with them. Business Connector is mostly used for peer-to-peer connections whereas XI is a central integration hub.

☞ QUESTION 74

Need XML File From Business Connector

I want to write a program that parses the XML file generated from the business connector. The problem is our Business Connector does not work at the moment and we cannot create a XML File. What is the structure of the generated XML?

✍ ANSWER

You should have the DTD or Schema available. Either the Business Connector is passing the IDOC file (see transaction code WE60) or it is being mapped to another format. The SAP Business Connector does not make any changes itself.

☞ **QUESTION 75**

Fails Because Material Is Locked

I have been working with an RFC that creates a Material Reservation in SAP via transaction code MB21. Basically, the RFC receives the data from the external program, creates the BDC internal tables and then runs a BDC session to create the reservation. When the material is locked (in use by another user) and the RFC is executed remotely, the BDC session will fail causing the RFC to also fail. When the material is locked and I test the RFC via transaction code SE37 Single Test, it executes successfully. Why this is happening and how I can resolve the problem?

✍ **ANSWER**

I would start by finding the message number that the RFC call returns, by running a find in your RFC function module. If it is not in the RFC function module, it will probably be in the MB21 transaction code. You may run a "where used" on the message in transaction code SE91 to find out where it is used.

Once you find out where it is, you can then start determining why it is only happening when called remotely. It probably has something to do with the manner that the function is run (i.e. foreground versus background mode).

In addition, take time to review OSS note 335598.

☞ QUESTION 76

IDOC File For Condition Type Pricing Upload

There is a requirement to upload Condition Type based prices into SAP. For this the IDOC file Type 685_01 was identified. However this IDOC file does not seem to have a message type or function module associated with it. If I must migrate prices based on condition type (similar to transaction MEK1), which IDOC file should be used?

✍ ANSWER

To solve this problem apply message type COND_A, IDOC file type COND_A02. I remember Application Link Enabling pricing conditions between clients at a past client. I think this is standard functionality within one of the pricing transactions (not in the Application Link Enabling area menu).

☞ QUESTION 77

Date .. Is Not Valid" Error

While calling Bapi_Salesorder_Createfromdat2 generated by SAP .NET Connector 1.2 to create an order, I receive an error "Date .. is not valid". Calling the same function from SAP GUI does not require any date. All dates in the tables I passed were optional. I filled date fields in headerIn and ItemsIn parameters but I am receiving the same error. I have tried different formats with the same results. How should I correct this error?

✍ ANSWER

If you set the debug mode on the proxy your debugging will also run in debug mode for the ABAP Code and you can see the SAP code run as well. But, this cannot be done for an ASP. net page. It must be run in a C# or Visual Basic application.

☞ **QUESTION 78**

Are RFC Functions Safe?

I would like to use RFC functions to import data from SAP to other applications. Is it possible to corrupt SAP R/3 using standard SAP RFC functions incorrectly?

✍ **ANSWER**

If you are implementing standard BAPI functions like BAPI_SALES_ORDER_CREATE_FROM DAT2, then you cannot damage SAP any more than you would if you entered data manually in the transaction.

☞ **QUESTION 79**

BAPI and Business Connector

I have created a new BAPI in the R3 system and I want to use it through the Business connector. Should I add it in a new package and folder or do something in the Business Connector Developer?

✍ **ANSWER**

You should add an inbound routing rule on the Business Connector server, by putting in the BAPI name. Use SAP Adapter under Business Connector administrator (http://yourIShost:5555) and look up your RFC enabled function module.

☞ QUESTION **80**

BAPI Function Module Help

I am attempting to use BAPI function module BAPI_CATIMESHEETMGR_INSERT. Are there examples that I can look at on how to use the function module or any documentation available on the subject?

✍ ANSWER

You can find a more detailed explanation under the SAP interface repository located at http://ifr.sap.com - Component:SAP HR - Hierarchy:CA,TimeSheet - Instance Method:CATimeSheetManager.Insert.

Depending on the function module calling methodology, you may also use the class method directly to the function module.

☞ QUESTION 81

Skip Records In LSMW & Transfer It To A Different File

I need to skip a record in LSMW and transfer the skipped records to another file so that I can keep track of all the skipped records. How would I do this?

✍ ANSWER

At the point that you decide you do not want this record (in the conversion program/step), use skip_record or skip_ transaction to prevent output of that record. Use the write command to generate your report. You can then use the transfer command to output this record to the application server. Or create an internal table, append the record, and at the end of processing, output the table via wsdownload/ gui_download to output to the presentation server.

☞ QUESTION 82

BAPI In 40B To Create Sales Order

Is there a BAPI, program or function module that can validate all items for a given order and then create a sales order containing only the items not flagged due to error and exclude the rejected items? And is there a way to simulate all items at once rather than one at a time?

✍ ANSWER

Try implementing the program BAPI_SALESORDER_ SIMULATE.

☞ **QUESTION 83**

Download To RFC Destination

I want to download an internal table/flat file using RFC to a particular RFC destination directory. How can I do this?

✍ ANSWER

You can use RFC_READ_TABLE from a different system into your SAP system to read a table.

☞ **QUESTION 84**

IDOC File Size

We are currently sending out IDOC files into another subsystem. The subsystem allocates a maximum of 100MB and we are experiencing some problems since we are exporting extremely large IDOC file. Knowing the IDOC file size will allow us to evaluate memory allocation in the subsystem. Is there any way to view the actual IDOC file size that was generated from our source system?

✍ **ANSWER**

Re-send the IDOC file (transaction code WE19 test tool) to a file port destination and view the size of the file.

☞ **QUESTION 85**

IDOC File ORDERS01

Does anyone know if the segment E1EDP03 is customizable? When we create the order response, we receive line items dates E1EDP03 022, 023, 025 and 026. What we really need is the requested delivery date E1EDP03 002. However, this segment is not generated for us. How can I receive this information?

✍ **ANSWER**

In most systems, the requested delivery date comes out at header level, i.e. E1EDK03 IDDAT= 002. You should find it there. If your customer gives you a delivery date at item level and you load this into the schedule lines, then you probably need to code the change in the order response yourself. Use customer function EXIT_SAPLVEDC_002 to code the ABAP, read the dates and fill E1EDP03.

☞ **QUESTION 86**

Goods Receipt Via EDI/IDOC File

I need to post a goods receipt to a consignment location via EDI. I will be receiving an INVRPT from the consignment location when they receive the goods from our supplier. We are not responsible for ordering the parts so there are no orders/schedule lines in our system. What IDOC file would be best to accomplish this task?

✍ **ANSWER**

The appropriate IDOC file would be WMMBID02, message type WMMBXY. This code applies to all movement types.

☞ **QUESTION 87**

Application Link Enabling Problem With Internal Order

Which message type and process code can be used in replicating internal orders through Application Link Enabling?

✍ **ANSWER**

You may replicate internal orders by implementing the InternalOrder.SaveReplica BAPI on the outbound side and the INTERNAL_ORDER message type (with process code BAPI) on the inbound side to Application Link Enabling internal orders. Unfortunately, you will not be able to edit the internal order on the receiving system. For a workaround, please check SAP NOTE 182140.

☞ QUESTION 88

Date Values To Segment E1EDK03

I need to include a new date value to segment E1EDK03. The standard IDOC file type ORDERS05 (purchase document) provides two kinds of dates: 011 and 012. I want to use 022. How I can do this?

✍ ANSWER

Without knowing what type of document you are sending (E1EDK03 occurs in lots of IDOC file types), it is hard to say exactly what user exit to use. You should look in the function module that creates and sends the IDOC file to find a user exit that will do the job.

Outbound purchase order documents use function module IDOC_OUTPUT_ORDERS. You would probably use customer function EXIT_SAPLEINM_002. You should create a project for enhancement MM06E001 in CMOD and then code the user exit.

Your code might look something like this:

(declare w_e1edk03, w_first and w_somedate in the function group top include)
CASE int_edidd-segnam.
WHEN 'E1EDK01'.
w_first = 'X'. " flag first segment
WHEN 'E1EDKA1'.
* insert E1EDK03 segment before the first E1EDKA1 segment
if w_first = 'X'.
w_first = ''.

```
clear w_E1EDK03.
W_E1EDK03-IDDAT = "022".
W_E1EDK03-DATUM = w_somedate.
MOVE W_E1EDK03 TO int_edidd-sdata.
MOVE 'E1EDK03' to int_edidd-segnam.
APPEND int_edidd.
ENDCASE.
```

☞ **QUESTION 89**

Information Message In IDOC File

During normal sales order posting from Va01 I am receiving information and warning messages. Now I am creating sales order via inbound IDOC file. Can I capture these messages at any point since I am not receiving these messages in IDOC file?

✍ **ANSWER**

The messages from the call transaction go into the internal table xbdcmsgcoll which you can then read in EXIT_SAPLVEDA_003 which is in IDOC_INPUT_ORDERS as:

* additional checks after call transaction VA01
CALL CUSTOMER-FUNCTION '003'
EXPORTING
sales_document = belegnummer
docnum = idoc_contrl-docnum
TABLES
didoc_data = idoc_data
dbdcmsgcoll = xbdcmsgcoll
CHANGING
status = ok.

☞ **QUESTION 90**

Application Link Enabling Segment

I am attempting to create a new segment under a segment (E1ELD24)---->E1ELDL41 at the same level. I also need to create a copy of 41 at same level under 24. How should I execute this?

✍ **ANSWER**

Create a new segment thru WE31 transaction code and add the fields. Then go to transaction code WE30, create an object type and add your segment to that object.

SAP does not allow you to directly add a segment to the existing segments. You must create an object first then add this object to the existing segments.

☞ QUESTION 91

SAP To VB

I am writing a program where I am receiving the data from different table that I then send to VB. In VB, there will be some modifications and the data will be sent to SAP.

What are the prerequisites for communication from SAP to VB and how should I write the RFC?

✍ ANSWER

First, write a RFC to fetch the data from different tables. Next, write another RFC that accepts the modified values from VB. Call the first RFC from VB, so you will receive the records in a table. Manipulate the data on VB and populate the TABLE of the second RFC. Then call the RFC.

You can also use DCOM connector to connect from VB to SAP. There are many other ways to do this.

☞ **QUESTION 92**

Connect From Delphi To Sap RFC Function

We created a function that receives strings as input and return strings as output. We have a problem using the function from our Delphi program based on librfc32.dll. Other system functions like "RFC_PING" are working. What is the problem?

✍ **ANSWER**

Make sure that you have made the function RFC by selecting the check box. If that is not the problem attempt to define the DATAELEMENT/DOMAIN for the import parameter.

☞ QUESTION 93

Programs To Send IDOC Files To Ext Sys

I am attempting to find programs to send IDOC files to external systems. I have found some programs. But I am unable to find programs for the following IDOC files:

LOIBOM
LOIROU
LOIWCS
LOIRNH
LOISTD
LOIMSO
LOIPLO
CLFMAS
BATMAS
LOICAL

✍ ANSWER

All of these message types are related to master data. If they are, then you can use RBDMIDOC file to generate outbound IDOC files. But one catch is that you need to configure change pointers. If you do, this program is the best.

You can find programs to dispatch the IDOC files for message types LOXXXX
in transaction SCPI

RBDMCCOP ==> for LOISTD
RCCLMDAT ==> for master data

☞ **QUESTION 94**

RFC Destination - Activation Type Registration

We are attempting to create an RFC Destination of type TCP/IP using Registration as the activation type. We need to specify the Program ID that an external system will use to register to SAP. Where exactly is this Program Id used?

✍ ANSWER

Normally, you set up a listener in the system that will process the RFC requests (such as business connector). When you create a listener, you assign it a program ID. The listener then registers itself with the SAP system using the program ID. Whenever you create an RFC destination using the program ID, it will look for a registered listener with the same program ID and use the corresponding TCP/IP port to perform the request.

☞ **QUESTION 95**

Debugging During IDOC File Generation

I am using IDOC_OUTPUT_ORDERS to perform processing during creation of an IDOC file and I want to debug the piece of code written.

How can I debug my code?

✍ **ANSWER**

If you are using IDOC_OUTPUT_ORDERS, then you are probably using ME21N or ME22N to create or change a PO to generate the output. The output type for purchase orders is normally NEU.

Go into ME22N for the PO you are sending and go to the menu Go to - messages. Select the NEU EDI output and choose repeat output. This will create a new line for NEU that is ready to send. Select this line and go into "further data". Change the dispatch time to "Send with periodically scheduled job". Save the PO.

Go into your user exit and set a break point.

Now go to transaction code SE38, run program RSNAST00. Put in parameters:

Output application: EF
Object key: your PO number
output type: NEU
transmission medium: 6

When you execute the code, your breakpoint should be hit. You may continue to run this code and select "send again" if you want to do this multiple times.

☞ QUESTION **96**

Decimal Point In IDOC Files

In generating invoice IDOC files (INVOIC02) I find a decimal point is used despite the settings of the user running the job being "comma" and the invoices being for a company which has a "comma" using country defined on the company file. How do I obtain commas in the IDOC file?

✐ ANSWER

The reason that you have a decimal is that the data in an IDOC file is held in the internal format. The user preferences only come into play as you display the data in SAP. With IDOC files, point is used as decimal separator and dates are formatted as follows: YYYYMMDD.

☞ QUESTION 97

Status Record

I am searching for all possible messages that appear in a status record, below status numbers. I found out that all messages are stored in table T100. But there is other data besides messages that are used in IDOC files, so I am not sure how to determine which is which. How should I solve this problem?

✍ ANSWER

EDIDS is the IDOC file status record table. A status record can contain any error message in T100, because the IDOC file function modules create status table entries, and there is no limitation on what messages can be created.

If you want past status messages, you can look in EDIDS, if you want all messages that could possibly occur, then T100 is the table. If you are just doing this for something like orders, you could go through the IDOC_INPUT_ORDERS function module to see what error message ids are used.

☞ **QUESTION 98**

IDOC_input_orders

When using forwarding agents, I use E1EDKA1-PARVW with CR, but now that I have upgraded my system it seems I must use SP. Is there some customization I must implement?

✍ **ANSWER**

Using SP is a good choice. If you look at domain EDIF3035 in transaction code SE11, you can view the values you can choose in the "Value range" tab.

☞ **QUESTION 99**

How To Obtain File List In Business Connector

Is there a standard Business Connector service to obtain names of files in a folder? I must obtain data from an XML file but I do not know the name of this file.

✍ **ANSWER**

The only standard possibility inside Business Connector is to use the service pub.client.ftp:ls. Otherwise, you must build up an FTP scenario.

☞ QUESTION 100

How To Configure Partner File For Inbound Process

I want to create sales orders by using IDOC file. But when I use transaction code WE19 to test the IDOC file, it does not know how to configure the control record for sending and receiving.

✍ ANSWER

Have you defined your sender and receiver ports in transaction code WE21, and set up the partner profile in transaction code WE20? If you have done this, then you should have most of the fields you need in the control record. If not, then your IDOC file will not work.

☞ QUESTION 101

Unprocessed IDOCs

We are having a problem in which the number of sales order IDOCs created for the day are not being processed (sent to the recipient) within the day. How do we fix this problem?

✍ ANSWER

You can batch these by modifying the message type in transaction code WE20 and setting 'Collect' option on. The appropriate programs need to be scheduled to process these. The programs in question are identified if you hit F1 in the field that identifies whether the IDOCs are collected.

☞ QUESTION 102

Sending Back an IDOC

Is there a standard way customer specific IDOCs can be sent and then sent back without any changes to be sent to the EDI sender system?

✍ ANSWER

Run transaction code WE81 to check the SAP standard message types.

☞ QUESTION 103

Status 03 With IDOC

All our partner profiles have now been set to collect IDOCs as opposed to transferring document immediately. However, now we start off at status 30, move to status 03 and eventually end up at status 41. However, should status 03 records eventually be set to zero? Why does the count against various message types within status 03 not equal zero? Also, what exactly does status 39 really mean and how can I reprocess these?

✍ ANSWER

Status 39 through 41 is the status of the IDOCs in the receiving system. They are set by ALEUD IDOCs. To change the status you have to process the IDOC in receiving system and send another ALEUD back to the sending system. It is better to monitor the IDOC in the receiving system.

☞ QUESTION 104

Status 51 Records

We show a fair number of status 51 records, which are the result of some kind of locking. What is causing this lock or what table is actually being locked?

✍ ANSWER

The Z program that creates the IDOCs is causing the lock. Revisit the locking methods used by this code.

☞ QUESTION 105

Inbound Delivery

When I post a goods receipt for the inbound delivery (transaction VL032N) with movement type 101 for the unrestricted use stock through IDOC WMMBID02 (message type WMMBXY), the system does not post any goods receipt. The system displays the following error message in the IDOC status: Update control of movement type incorrect (entry 101 X X _ _ _ G). How would I fix this?

✍ ANSWER

In message type WMMBXY, field KZBEW must have been set to "B" since the inbound delivery serves as a path for finding the purchase order. The purchase order is updated constantly, but not the inbound delivery. Thus, no posting documents are created for the inbound delivery. Furthermore, you should use transaction MB0A instead of VL32N.

☞ Question 106

Goods Movement With EDI

If a goods movement is posted with EDI for the shipping notification by IDOCs, the system always updates the first shipping notification (ASN) even though the external delivery number (E1MBXYH-XBLNR) is uniform. ASN (=Advanced Shipment Notification), table for that: XKOMDLGN

How do we correct this?

✍ Answer

In order to have the correct shipping notification (ASN) pulled, it is necessary that fields VLIEF_AVIS and VBELP_ AVIS are filled. The purchase order number and the purchase order item must not be filled here. The IDOC is a technical interface which does not pull the "correct" ASN itself. It must have all necessary data so that it can pull the correct ASN. If this is not the case, it will always pull the first item.

☞ Question 107

No Error Message Issued With R/3

Why does the R/3 not issue any error message with a difference in material number/name between the IDOC and the inbound delivery/purchase order?

✍ Answer

This system response is normal. The IDOC "does not think." It is merely filled with data that it then issues again (example: inbound delivery, purchase order). The system assumes that the IDOC is filled correctly. The material field in the IDOC has been designed so that a material number is specified (example movement type 301). For conventional posting with reference to the purchase order, the material number is pulled from the purchase order item and not externally.

☞ QUESTION **108**

Goods Receipt Error Message

During the attempt to post a goods receipt for the purchase order via the IDOC, the system displays error message M3351. However, the material has actually been maintained. What could be the problem?

✍ ANSWER

You must fill the IDOC with the internal display of the material number, thus in the same way as the material number is saved on the database. The IDOC does not take the conversion exit into account. This means that you must fill field material number with leading zeros (that is, for example, 00000000001100300). You should also fill field KZBEW with 'B' (for purchase order).

☞ QUESTION 109

Field LFSNR

Why is field LFSNR (number of the external delivery note) not filled for a goods receipt posting with function module L_IDOC_INPUT_WMMBXY? How can this field be filled via the MOB interface?

✍ ANSWER

For this field XBLNR is to be filled in structure E1MBXYH.

☞ QUESTION 110

Reservation Updating

A goods movement with reference to a reservation is posted via the IDOC WMMBID01/WMMBXY. Why is updating of the reservation incorrect?

✍ ANSWER

For example, the final issue indicator has been set even though the quantity withdrawn is smaller by the requirement quantity of the reservation. A termination of the IDOC occurs if the reservation and the item are transferred, if they do not exist and if the reservation should not be read, that is, flag XRERE is blank. The reason for the error is that the interface for function module MB_CREATE_GOODS_MOVEMENT has been filled incorrectly. The reservation is read at the time of the IDOC creation. You must fill the fields in structure E1MBXYI: RSNUM, RSPOS, RSART, KZEAR, BDMNG, RSHKZ, ENMNG. If the reservation is not to be read, the initiator must make sure that this exists. If this is not the case, a termination occurs upon the attempt to update a non-existing reservation.

☞ QUESTION 111

Specified Unit of Measure Not Defined

During processing of an IDOC, the system issues error message MM107 (Specified alternative unit of measure is not defined).

What cold be causing this?

✍ ANSWER

IDOCs of message type WMMBXY that are updated by function module L_IDOC_INPUT_WMMBXY expect the specification of units of measure in the SAP internal format. If you want to transfer units in ISO codes, you must activate SAP enhancement MWMIDO08 through transaction code CMOD. You must insert the specified call of function module UNIT_OF_MEASURE_ISO_TO_SAP in exit function module EXIT_SAPLLMDE_002 for every quantity field that you use in the IDOC.

☞ **QUESTION 112**

Error Message M7073

When I post a goods movement with reference to the sales order or the project stock with IDOC WMMBXY, the system displays error message M7073 (Please enter a sales order for special stock). If I post a goods movement through the dialog, no error message is issued. Why is this?

✍ **ANSWER**

You must fill in the fields KDAUF, KDPOS, PS_PSP_PNR, MAT_KDAUF, MAT_KDPOS and MAT_PSPNR as described in note 307731.

☞ QUESTION 113

Bar Code

If I post a goods movement with an IDOC or a BAPI and I have set "S" for this movement type or user and active the bar code entry, a dialog box is also sent for this processing in order to enter the bar code. With processing in the background, specifying or filling of the bar code is not possible so that the goods movement cannot be posted. How do I resolve this issue?

✎ ANSWER

In order not to allow any bar code entry for batch input or IDOC processing, there are some steps you must take. In customizing, activate the Archive Link (via transaction code OAC5) for the respective user with which the batch input or the IDOC is run. Next, deactivate the bar code entry (refer to note 453920).

☞ QUESTION 114

Evaluating Translation Software

I need to evaluate EDI translation software? What are the pros and cons of some of the software available?

✍ ANSWER

XI Version 2 does not support SSL. With XI, there are extra licensing charges per each non-SAP connection, which will cost you extra. Gentran is suitable for EDI interfaces, but the Gentran Integration Suite that supports XML does have some technical bugs. WBI from IBM is also reliable for integrating SAP.

☞ QUESTION 115

IDOC Retry Counter

Our IDOCs retry once every 15 minutes for up to 20 attempts when sending to the recipient. Where is this configured and how we can modify this?

✍ ANSWER

Check RFC connection under transaction code SM59. Open connection and from menu destination item TRFC options configure there.

☞ QUESTION 116

Status 03 records

I have switched on 'suppress background job if conn.error' and now the 'connection attempts' and 'time' is now no longer an option. I have IDOCs being processed in batch (status 30) but I am alarmed at the number of status 03's records that still exist. I thought these were converted to status 30, but although status 30 records are being produced, I still have an increasing number of status 03 records. Can you explain how these 03 status records can be processed?

✍ ANSWER

This is the order for outbound IDOCs. First status 01, IDOCs are created. Second status 30, IDOCs are ready for dispatch. Third status 03, data is passed to port. Fourth status 12 dispatch is okay. This is optional. You would need to run RBDMOIND and further status depending on your ALEAUD information returned from target system. Status 03 will never switch to status 30, but status 30 will switch to status 03.

☞ QUESTION 117

Sending Data to Multiple Systems

We want to send data to multiple logical systems with one IDOC. However, we cannot configure two receiving systems for the same message type. What is a solution to this?

✎ ANSWER

You can send the same IDOC type to different logical system provided you have configured the distribution model correctly in BD64. The way SAP can send the same IDOC to a different logical system is that it reads all the partners for that particular message type and then distributes it to the respective systems. Check that there are not filters active that might prevent the IDOC from being distributed to the other system.

☞ QUESTION **118**

Partner profile configuration

We are setting up partner profiles for customers so we can accept inbound sales orders .In the incoming parameters, must the partner role be 'BP', 'SH', 'WE' and so on for each customer or is one sufficient? If one is sufficient, how will the system handle it?

✍ ANSWER

You will only be able to successfully post if what is sent in the control record matches the partner profile. If they do not match the IDOC will fail with a status 56. Limit the number of partner profiles that you create to control the amount of maintenance. Set them up by sold-to (partner function AG/ SO) and send the ship to information in the KA1 segments.

☞ **QUESTION 119**

Outbound Records

I have recently changed my IDOCs to be processed in batch (collect IDOCs set within transaction code WE20). I have also changed my ALEAUD IDOCs to be processed in background. These are being controlled by period execution of programs RBDAPP1 and RSEOUT00. I am concerned that the number of status 03 records is growing. I have always understood that the status 30 records replaced status 03?

✐ **ANSWER**

In actuality, it is the reverse. For outbound records, when the IDOCs is created by the application, it goes to status 30 waiting to be passed to the port if the partner profile is set to 'collect IDOCs.' If you run RSEOUT00 and it is successful it goes to 03. This should be the final status unless your subsystem software is configured to send back additional statuses.

☞ QUESTION **120**

Mapping IDOCs to EDI

What are the functional specifications that will be needed for mapping IDOCs to EDI?

✍ ANSWER

You can find out the specifications by looking at a document from SAP called "analysis of the compatibility of edifact messages in SIMPL-EDI with the IDOC interface".

☞ QUESTION 121

Missing IDOC

One of our customers does not create an IDOC automatically to send an 856 ASN. Why is this happening?

✍ ANSWER

The reason why it is not creating an IDOC automatically is because the delivery is not packed. The warehouse did not generate the MH10 label as a requirement for advance shipping notice.

☞ QUESTION 122

IDOC for Sales Order Missing Information

I have a requirement to create an IDOC for sales order history. I created output type and partner profiles. I am using message type ORDRSP and IDOC type ORDERS05 with process code SD10. This creates an IDOC whenever sales order is changed, but the history or invoice number is not populated in the IDOC. Am I missing something in the configuration? Is it possible to create an IDOC for sending sales order history?

✍ ANSWER

Working in the sales order will only give you sales order information with standard IDOCs. There are two ways to approach this problem.

Continue using what you have but code a user exit to get the information that is missing. Work with the invoice and configure message type INVOIC and process transaction code SD09. You will get the sales order number and delivery number in segments E1EDP02 along with the invoice number in E1EDK01.

☞ **QUESTION 123**

Extracting Data From EDI 830

I have the requirement to get a field from EDI 830 (Inbound). How can I get the corresponding IDOC type and message type?

✍ **ANSWER**

The message type for EDI830 is DELFOR, and its corresponding IDOC type is DELFOR 01.

☞ QUESTION **124**

BAPI For Repetitive Manufacturing Component Entry

Is there a BAPI or method for entering repetitive manufacturing backflush with component usage modifications?

✍ ANSWER

SAP states the functionality of the BAPI is not fully implemented, meaning it does not yet fully emulate the MFBF transaction (which enters repetitive manufacturing backflush made to stock). Currently the BAPI only allows the assembled product with quantity to be entered, not the components.

☞ QUESTION 125

Conversion From IDOC to XML Using BC

How would I go about converting IDOCs to XML using BC and vice versa?

✍ ANSWER

IDOC can be converted to XML format in BC using XSL. You can use XSLT services in SAP: PUB: XSLT to convert XML format to an IDOC and send across to the SAP system.

☞ QUESTION 126

Business Connectors

What business connector services are used to process inbound orders? The service should read a file in IDOC format and generate an IDOC.

✍ ANSWER

When an IDOC comes into BC from SAP, you can use XSL to convert it to XML format. Similarly for outgoing IDOCs from BC, they can be converted from XML format to IDOCs using XSLT services in SAP: PUB: XSLT: Transformations.

☞ QUESTION 127

Purchase Order EDI

When creating or changing the purchase order system it automatically creates the message type NEU.

We set up the EDI configuration and in one case E1EDKA1 segment displays plant and plant name instead of customer address. I want to perform a debugging. Where should I set up the breakpoint?

✍ ANSWER

Output determination in purchase orders are done as a separate background process, not in the dialog process. You must repeat NEU in ME22N output but set the timing to one and send with periodically scheduled job. Set breakpoint in IDOC_OUTPUT_ORDERS, and then go to SE38 and execute program RSNAST00 with the following parameters:

application: EF
object key: [your po number]
output type: NEU
transmission medium: 6 (for edi) or A (for ALE)

When you execute this, your breakpoint will stop and you will be able to perform a debugging.

☞ **QUESTION 128**

Copying a Flow Service in Business Connector

I am copying a flow service from one folder to another. I do not want to change the name. The BC says that a flow service already exists with the package folder name even though it does not. How can I get around this obstacle?

✍ **ANSWER**

The relationship between the package name and the folder name can cause confusion. The name of the package to which a service belongs has no bearing on the names of the services and folders it contains, nor does it affect how it is referenced by a client application. For example, if you move a service called "Personnel:GetDeptNames" from a package called "Admin.," to a package called "EmployeeData," you will not affect client applications that reference that service—it will still be referenced by the name "Personnel:GetDepNames."

Because the fully qualified name of each service must be unique within the server, you cannot have two identically named services in two different packages on the same server. You can copy that service from another folder prod: invoice:inv001 and paste it into ur dev:invoice . This way it will be copied as inv001 copy1. However, if you try to create a new flow service with the same name inv001 after deletion of existing flow service in dev:invoice, bc will not allow you to create with the same name as a flow service as the same name already exists in prod:invoice folder.

☞ QUESTION **129**

Transaction Code BDA1 Not Working

I'm running transaction BDA1 to execute IDOCs and force processing status from 03 to 41 for sales orders, but nothing happens. If I were to reprocess these records one at a time via transaction code SM58, then these records are processed properly. Why are these records are not being processed?

✍ ANSWER

You should change the 'no records later than' field from '00:30:00' to '00:00:00' when in BDA1 transaction.

☞ QUESTION **130**

Cannot Assign Function Module to an Event Code

I need to assign a Function Module to an already existing event code. However, the function module is not present in the pull down table. The import parameters are present in the Function Module. How would I solve this problem?

✍ ANSWER

In order to assign a function module to an event code, you must first add the function module in transaction code BD51.

☞ QUESTION 131

XML and SAP Interface

A customer wants data transferred from our nonpublic SQL-server. This needs to be transmitted in XML. How can a document be integrated into SAP?

✍ ANSWER

There are several components that can receive XML and transfer it to SAP. Among others, the most utilized methods are SAP Business Connector, Java Connector, Exchange Infrastructure, DCOM connector and .NET connector.

Extract data from your database and format it to previously agreed (with customer) XML standard and send it to your customer by HTTP(S), FTP or e-mail. The most important thing is to agree upon XML standard and matching master records. When connector receives XML document it will transform it to SAP readable format and transmit it to SAP via BAPI or IDOC.

You must decide upon way of transformation from file produced by your database to XML file. It is not important that SAP is on the other side. Send the XML file to address given by your customer.

☞ QUESTION 132

Classification View

Which material master IDOC type can handle classification view also? I am developing an interface to send material master classification data to the legacy system. If material master does not have classification view, does another IDOC have this available?

✍ ANSWER

The creation of classification view in material master can be done through CLFMAS not through material master (Classification of object: MARA).

☞ QUESTION 133

BAPI and SNC

We need to call a BAPI from VB, but the SNC is creating a problem. We are not able to get through once we enable the SNC login. How can we resolve this issue?

✍ ANSWER

You must declare "RfcOpenEx" and use it. If you would like to go with the standard logon dialog, you have to make an error, catch it, then continue. Or you can write a dialog by yourself and call "RfcOpenEx" directly, so that you won't see any error message.

☞ QUESTION **134**

More Than One Extension in IDOC

Can an IDOC type have more than one extension for the same message type?

✍ ANSWER

Yes, it is possible for an IDOC type to have more than one extension for the same message type.

☞ QUESTION 135

Conde_A Message

I need to send pricing info from a purchase order to another SAP system. Is it possible to use a COND_A message?

✍ ANSWER

First you will have to create logical system in which you will send the pricing records. Then go to transaction code MEK3, enter condition type and press "Condition Info." Here you can restrict your selection on the available filters and then execute to get the list of condition records to be transferred. Then select all the condition records and click "Send condition." In the pop-up, enter message type as "COND_A" and the logical system created.

☞ **QUESTION 136**

Uploading IDOCs

I have an IDOC in quality and production. I need similar IDOCs in development for testing. I have downloaded the contents of the IDOC on my desktop from a quality server through transaction code WE09. Is there any other way to copy IDOCs from quality to development server?

✍ **ANSWER**

Follow these steps. Go to a server and find an IDOC that you want to use as a template. Display the IDOC using WE19.

Click on the inbound file and type in a file name. Make sure the option 'Start inbound IDOC processing of the file immediately' is unchecked. Choose overwrite file, then click the tick. This will write an IDOC into the AL11 directory structure in the system you are operating in. Using the download and upload functions (CG3Z & CG3Y), transfer the file to the production AL11 directories. Use transaction code WE19 to process your downloaded IDOC. Use the option 'File as template' to pick up your file. You should now be able to process your IDOC as you wish.

☞ QUESTION 137

EAN Numbers

When we get EAN numbers coming in from our customers, it looks in SAP and finds two materials with the same EAN number. Reports such as ABAP can be written to show two materials with same EAN number (SQ01 etc.), but surely this needs to be fixed without the need of running reports. What can be done about this issue?

✍ ANSWER

To avoid duplicate EAN numbers go to transaction code OMT4 and make the error message number 348 either a warning or an error.

☞ QUESTION **138**

Sales Order Change in IDOC

I want to send sales order change details out in IDOC format (ORDERS05). Are there any standard process codes available? How can I do this?

✍ ANSWER

If you want to send the sales order change information and if the message control is configured, it can be sent in the form of an IDOC. It can be triggered using message output (as we use for script output), and you can resend the output. The base for this is the configuration of message control output.

☞ QUESTION **139**

Creating Output Type For Material Management

I'm creating an output type which linked the program: RSNASTED & Form Routine: EDI_PROCESSING with transmission medium six. However IDOCs cannot be created when the system is trying to process this output type but instead I receive an error message that states, "No entry for partner in table TPAR". What should I do to fix the problem?

✍ **ANSWER**

Set up the correct partner profile via transaction code WE20.

☞ **QUESTION 140**

IDOC With Message Type DESADV

I'd like to know how to create an IDOC, message type DESADV?

✍ **ANSWER**

Open your delivery document in change mode (VL02N). Go to header output.

Create an output type LAVA with media 6 EDI. This assumes that you have set correctly the partner profile in transaction code WE20.

☞ **QUESTION 141**

SAP Interface Options For Synchronous Transactions

I have to look for potential options to interface our SAP System to another shipping system. The interface between the two systems is required to be synchronous. It shall both upload and download from the other system. Is BAPI the only viable solution? I understand that IDOCs are asynchronous and hence not suitable in this case. What should I do about this problem?

✐ **ANSWER**

The standard synchronous solution for EDI is BAPI. IDOCs are asynchronous, but that doesn't mean poor performance. If you connect through RFC, you only have a few seconds between the time you send the IDOC and the time it is processed. Error processing is asynchronous and the caller cannot be sure the process has been successful. If you want to use BAPI, list them up with the BAPI transaction and evaluate them with the test tool. Be careful about the commit issues when doing this.

☞ QUESTION 142

SAP XI

My understanding is that the SAP XI integration platform is only available with the latest version of SAP (SAP Netweaver). We have version 4.6 in place. Can we still look at SAP XI as a potential integration platform, or is this out of the picture, as we do not have the latest version of SAP?

✍ ANSWER

The program XI can be used independent of the SAP version. As long as you can set up a logical system and RFC destination, you can use XI.

☞ QUESTION 143

Literal Values For the Qualifiers

For mapping, where can I get the literal values for the qualifiers?

✍ ANSWER

Go to transaction code SE11, enter EDI_QUALFO in domain field and display, then select value range tab.

☞ **QUESTION 144**

Transferring Hierarchies Between Clients

I am currently investigating using the ALE IDOCs to transfer accounting hierarchies between clients. I am getting the below error message "Could not determine recipients for message type COGRP6" because the sender/receivers are not set up. What could be the problem?

✍ **ANSWER**

Maintain your distribution model; ensure that partner profile is set up properly. The distribution model can be maintained using the Transaction BD64.

You need to define the model view if the data is sent through message type. Place cursor on the newly created model view and then click on 'Add message type'. Give the sending and receiving system names (logical system names) and the message type. Save the contents.

☞ QUESTION 145

Insert Segment to IDOC

I have two segments, say, A1 and B1. I want to add the A1 segment to the IDOC and B1 as a child of A1. These two segments are already created. I am using 4.6c, and the IDOC is already set to Release. When I try to insert the segment A1 it says 'No segment types in the clipboard.' Is there any procedure to insert the segment?

✍ ANSWER

While creating the IDOC type with the segments created, give the IDOC type and click on create. In the new screen select the IDOC and click on create segment and give the segment name (Parent). Place the cursor on the Parent segment and again click on create segment. This time it will ask for segment hierarchy (add segment type as child or at same level). Select the appropriate button.

☞ QUESTION **146**

User Exit For Message Type Orders

I am creating a new segment. Now I am facing a problem while writing code to update data in this extension. I have inserted break points to trace the function exit but the system is not stopping anywhere, so I am not able to trace the accurate function where I can write a code for inserting the values.

✍ ANSWER

The easiest way is to find the function module attached to the process code (in inbound processing) for the IDOC type. The function module you are looking for is IDOC_INPUT_ ORDRSP. Search for the text 'CALL CUSTOMER_FUNCTION ' in the above function module. The break points can be put in these exits and you can find the appropriate exit where the code needs to be written.

☞ **QUESTION 147**

Distinguishing Sales Organizations

We are running SAP R/3 4.6 C (SP 46) with one client 010 and three companies, 0010, 0080, 0120 (each is a sales organization and a plant too).

We use IDOCs with basis type ORDERS05 to create sales orders for the subsidiaries. Due to not fully consolidated customer master data there are some IDOCs that will not be processed accordingly. In order to improve the diagnostics we need to distinguish the IDOCs from which subsidiary it was sent, to which sales organization it was addressed. How do we go about doing this?

✍ **ANSWER**

Find report with a data selection in edid4. Display in ALV, then call transaction code WE02 by BDCdata.

☞ QUESTION **148**

XML and SAP 4.6

How can we interface a non-SAP system with a SAP 4.6 system passing data using XML?

✍ ANSWER

Use XML class files or Business Connectors.

☞ QUESTION 149

Intercompany ALE/EDI Within Same Client

I'm trying to prototype an inter-company code ordering process utilizing IDOCs. Company A creates purchase orders and Company B fills it. We plan to utilize standard ORDERS/ORDERS05 outbound IDOC, and need to have the IDOC "boomerang" onto the same client as inbound and create a sales order. The inbound order will create a sales order on Company B. Both Company codes exist on the same system and client, so it is an intraclient ALE/EDI. Which RFC connection, port definition and partner profile definition is used for this scenario?

✍ ANSWER

Change the IDOC being generated from the purchase order to an inbound IDOC instead of the usual outbound. Create a new process code and assign in the partner profile. When you save the purchase order it will generate the IDOC and start the inbound process to create the sales order. You will have the purchase order and sales order in one step.

☞ QUESTION **150**

Creating A Qualifier Segment

I am trying to add a new date field to incoming orders. How can I create a qualifier for ORDERS05 - E1EDK03 segment?

✎ ANSWER

You can find this under EDI_IDDAT element definition.

☞ **QUESTION 151**

Determining Segment Responsible For Error

My IDOC is in status 51 and has more than 100 segments (one segment per employee). Is there a way to know which segment drives my IDOC to error?

✍ ANSWER

If you have access to ABAP repository objects, then you can access table EDIDS. Input the IDOC number and it will list out segment-wise errors within that IDOC.

☞ QUESTION 152

IDOC Hierarchy

Our IDOCs are not in our hierarchy. The SAP error message states, "EDI: Syntax error in IDOC (segment cannot be identified)." Where do we look to fix this problem?

✍ ANSWER

Transaction codes WE30 or WE31 will fix this problem. One pertains to the IDOC structure and the other refers to the field names within the segment.

☞ QUESTION 153

IDOC For Goods Receipt Note To Supplier

We are currently on SAP 4.5B and would like to make use of IDOCs via business connector to communicate to our suppliers. IDOCs for sending purchase orders and receiving invoices are in place and functioning well. However functionality for sending GRN information to supplier cannot be found. What should we do to fix this?

✍ ANSWER

The IDOC you are looking for is STPPOD (standard proof of delivery). The IDOC type is DELVRY03 and processing function is IDOC_OUTPUT_STPPOD. It is standard with inbound delivery functionality, but you will need to configure your SAP system for inbound deliveries if you want to use the OPOD output type that is the standard one. If you do not want to configure inbound deliveries, then you can set up a custom output type on the purchase order for the above message type.

☞ QUESTION 154

Article Master IDOC User Exit

If I extend the IDOC WPPLU then what will be the user exit used to populate the data into the new segment?

✍ ANSWER

Use the following to populate data into a new segment: EXIT_SAPLWPDA_002 (in 470).

☞ QUESTION 155

Marking IDOCs For Deletion

In my production system (SAP 4.6C), I have some inbound IDOCs that have the status 64 with an error message "unable to interpret a char. as number." I need to mark these IDOCs for deletion, or else find a way to correct them and get the status updated and process them via transaction code BD87. When I try to reprocess these IDOCs in transaction code BD87 a short dump occurs. How can I get around this error and mark these IDOCs for deletion?

✍ ANSWER

There are two ways to approach this. Go to transaction code BD87. Click on edit, then restrict and process. Do not flag background processing. Next click execute and delete flag. There is another way to solve this problem. There is a function module named EDI_DOCUMENT_DELETE. This deletes the IDOC and the entries in the corresponding tables.

☞ **QUESTION 156**

Sending Purchase Orders to Two Vendors

We have a requirement to send an EDI purchase order to a raw material vendor and the finished goods vendor from the same purchase order. I can manually create an output for both vendors but I need to automate the process. What is a method of doing so?

✍ **ANSWER**

In the output determination access sequence (get there via transaction NACE. Select "EF",and then click access sequences. Select your sequence, then double click access) there is a checkbox that tells whether a certain access is "exclusive." If this is left blank it means it will continue searching in other condition tables even after it finds a match. This means that you can have two NEU outputs set up. Another option is to create a new output type (again with NACE), say called ZNEU. This means that the two outputs can be handled independent of each other.

☞ QUESTION **157**

Processing Changed IDOCs

Is there a background job/process that picks up IDOCs with changed status and reprocesses them automatically?

✍ ANSWER

Instead of using transaction code WE19, you can also try transaction code BD87, this transaction allows you to post more than one IDOC at a time.

☞ QUESTION **158**

Recording Transaction QPV2

I have tried to make a recoding of transaction QPV2, but I have a problem. In the recording screen there is no dialog structure, which I need for entering more data about sample drawing items. When I enter data manually through transaction QPV2 I don't have such a problem. How can I get all the needed data with batch input?

✍ ANSWER

When recording in transaction SHDB the checkbox 'Not a Batch Input Session' should be checked. You also have to include BDCRECX1 and change the code. Next you must call your include instead of the standard one from your generated program.

☞ QUESTION 159

ALE Information in SAP Help 4.7

I am using SAP Help Version 4.7. I need info about master IDOCs, communication IDOCs, filtering, listing etc. What is the path of ALE information in SAP Help?

✍ ANSWER

Follow this path: Cross Application -> Business Framework Architecture-> ALE Business Process Library. Choose ALE quick start for an overview.

☞ QUESTION 160

Data Conversion On SAP Side

We are posting the IDOC ORDERS02 into SAP. The incoming IDOC will have the customer and material as per the external system. We need to convert the customer number and the material number as maintained in the SAP. We perform these conversions in the SAP side, not in the middleware. How do we convert the data?

✒ ANSWER

Transaction code VOE4 will take care of customer numbers. You can use transaction code VD51 for materials. You will only need the material number of the customer in the E1EDP19 segment with qualifier 001.

☞ QUESTION 161

Status Text

I have read the SAP note on how customers can define their own status values for the IDOC. In this description they use fields I do not have in my interface. How can I access the STA fields and use my own status texts?

✍ ANSWER

You must use your own message class and place it into the fields of BAPIRET2 . The IDOC status is set with these.

☞ **QUESTION 162**

IDOC Extension

I am having trouble extending an IDOC. I am trying to connect the extension I created and my custom segments with the basic IDOC type. What is the transaction code to get to the IDOC editor?

✍ **ANSWER**

In transaction code WE30 enter one Z IDOC name. Click on extension radio button and the create button. In the next screen it will ask you to create a copy from where you pass the basic type and description. Add your segment after this.

☞ QUESTION 163

Extracting Data

How do I extract data in order to retrieve data from the IDOC data file?

✍ ANSWER

For inbound testing purposes, you can go to transaction code WE19 (test tool) to populate data in the EDIDC record and data fields. Next, click on standard inbound to run the job. You must also have the partner profile and EDPAR/EDSDC table setup if you cross-reference.

☞ QUESTION **164**

EDI Interfacing

If a sales order message is received in the EDI subsystem, what is required in getting that data into SAP?

✍ ANSWER

Your trading partner will send you an EDI file in possibly an X12 format. Your middleware will translate the file from X12 format into IDOC format and then pass it on to SAP. You will then need to populate the data in EDIDC and EDIDATA. In SAP, you will need to create partner profile and other configuration depending on the type of transaction/document you want to bring in.

☞ **QUESTION 165**

Unable To Post Document

I am loading legacy master data from flat files to HR SAP using LSMW.

I am using an IDOC, message type HRMASTER, and basic type HRMASTER02. I am able to read data; LSMW.read is created and LSMW.conv is successful. The IDOCs are passed to the application, but the application document is not being posted and the IDOC status is 51. What steps do I take to fix this problem?

✍ **ANSWER**

Make sure that HR_OBJECT_HEADER has an entry for the object in question, and that HR_INFOTYPE_HEADER has an appropriate entry for the infotype.

☞ **QUESTION 166**

ALE Invoice

I am trying to send an INVOICE01 between the box of my system by ALE.

I can send the IDOC but an error occurs at the receiver box. The error is: Customer/vendor could not be determined for intermediate document 0000000003526927. What should I do to stop receiving this error message?

✍ **ANSWER**

Vendor and company code depend on the partner function you have chosen. If you have 'LF,' the vendor can be determined and is taken. The company code can be provided by the user exit EXIT_SAPLMRMH_011 in MRMH0002

☞ **QUESTION 167**

Logistics Invoice Verification

I configured a new output type and set up the condition records, but for some reason when I save the document it gives me an update error. Is it possible to set up the creation of an invoice IDOC when a logistics invoice is created using MIRO transaction?

✒ **ANSWER**

Use transaction code MRM2 to set up output on MIRO. Output type KON6 will work. Setup an outbound partner profile in WE20 for INVOIC/INVOIC02, with message control MR/KON6/SD09.

☞ QUESTION **168**

Copy CATTs Without Transport Request

I would like to copy CATT files from another server. I cannot use the transport request. How can I do this?

✍ ANSWER

You can remotely execute a CATT rather than transporting it. You will see a screen that asks for foreground, background etc. Click the "remote execution" button. You can then specify an RFC destination to execute your CATT. You can execute it in DEV, which will run the CATT in quality or production, for example.

☞ QUESTION 169

RFC Calls From .NET/Java Connector

I'm working in SAP CRM which has very few standard BAPIs. I have a need to read data and not write data. What is the process of calling function modules from these connectors?

✍ ANSWER

The functions need to be RFC enabled, which is found in the attributes section in transaction code SE37. Once they are enabled, you can call them like any other BAPI. If they are not RFC enabled, rather than change them you can write a wrapper function that is RFC enabled to call them.

☞ QUESTION 170

BOMMAT ISO Units

I am able to generate the BOMMAT03. In segment E1STPOM in field MEINS I have the ISO unit of measurement. Is there a user exit that can change this to a basic unit?

✐ ANSWER

SAP always uses ISO code units in IDOCs. It converts them by itself.

☞ **QUESTION 171**

EDI 834 Format

I am searching for an appropriate IDOC. I need an interface for third party vendors for benefits, what should I use?

✍ **ANSWER**

You can use IDOC type BENEFIT1, with logical message BENREP.

☞ QUESTION 172

Explaining EDI

How would you explain EDI?

✍ ANSWER

The term EDI is an acronym for Electronic Data Interchange. It refers to the movement of business data electronically between or within firms, in a structured format. It permits data to be transferred without reentering from a computer-supported business application in one location to a computer-supported business application in another location. It's a flat file format used to pass data, information, or records from one system to another. There are hundreds of different types of EDI's to handle different tasks.

☞ QUESTION 173

Starting SAPBC

I have a problem starting the SAPBC after using the new mail jar version 1.3. I am running SAPBC 4.6 with corefix4 under java j2sdk1.4.2_04. I need to implement the new mail 1.3 version to retrieve special mail from a mailbox. I have shut down the SAPBC and replaced the old version 1.2, with this new version. When I try to start the SAPBC I receive an error message. How do I resolve this?

✍ ANSWER

You can search for the file java.security under:
C:\j2sdk1.4.2_04\jre\lib\security\java.security)
Add the provider: iaik.security.provider.IAIK. This should solve the problem.

☞ **QUESTION 174**

Outbound IDOC with Status 26

I have added two segments in an extended IDOC. Basic IDOC type is invoic02. During the creation of an IDOC, it is showing status 26, segment unidentified. I have named the segments as Z1EDKA4 and Z1EDP26. I have also input the code in the user exit to populate those segments. What steps do I take to solve this?

✍ **ANSWER**

Specify the IDOC extension name in the outbound parameters of the receiving system under transaction code WE20, where you specified the message type.

☞ **QUESTION 175**

Partner Profile Error Message

I created two logical systems (log800, log900) in two different clients.

I want to send material master from one client to another client.

Both side's connections are working properly. I have created a model view and added the message type as well. My problem arises when I generate the partner profile; I keep receiving an error message. How do I solve this problem?

✍ **ANSWER**

You are most likely giving the wrong partner system name while generating partner profile. Generate the partner profile for LOG800 in LOG900.

☞ QUESTION **176**

Material Master IDOC and XML Through Change Pointers

We are distributing material master data through the concept of change pointers. Now we have the need to send material master data through IDOC but also in XML-format. The creation of material master, must lead to two output files. Is this possible in change pointers?

✐ ANSWER

If you create two reduced message types based on material master and turn the change pointers on for both of them, it will work perfectly. You can also add an ABAP to the user exit in sending material master IDOCs and duplicate them with the new control header. This method uses fewer pointers but is more work.

☞ QUESTION 177

Modifying Status Record

For inbound shipment, we have added preconditions in the user exit to fail an IDOC. In this user exit, we are raising the error. When it fails, status record shows no proper status message. In the user exit, the status record is not one of the parameters. Is there any way we can modify the status record?

✍ ANSWER

Modify the message in both tables; EDIDC (current status) and EDIDS (list of all status).

☞ QUESTION **178**

ALE Audit

We are sending an IDOC from one SAP system to the other via ALE. The client requires a report for the failed IDOC. In the receiving system if the IDOC fails while posting an application document they want this information in the sending system. The IDOC may be different in the receiving system. They would like both the sending IDOC and the receiving system IDOC in the report. How do we configure this?

✍ ANSWER

Use report RBDSTATE to create ALEAUD IDOCs. They include the status of received IDOCs and they are sent to the source system. After sending and processing ALEAUDs you can use transaction code BDM2 in the source system to track IDOCs and receive the IDOC numbers in the source and destination system.

☞ QUESTION 179

SYNCH Message Type

When configuring the ALE distribution model I receive an error message stating that the SYNCH message type is not configured. What must I do to resolve the issue?

✍ ANSWER

When you create a distribution model and the automatic partner function generation from transaction code BD64, the message type SYNCH is automatically added in the partner profile (outbound). You need SYNCH to send the distribution model to a target, system. In a target system you can easily create partner profile and port from transaction code BD64.

☞ QUESTION **180**

IDOC Type For RFQ

I am implementing EDI for RFQ as well as RFQ response. Which SAP IDOC type and message type is used for inbound quotation?

✍ ANSWER

Use REQOTE message and usual IDOC type like ORDERS01.

☞ **QUESTION 181**

Extending IDOC Material Master

As recommended by SAP notes, I am extending the basic type material master 03 of the message type material master. The extended IDOC type shall be named 'EXTMAT03'. How can I extend material master 03 IDOC type to include a new segment called 'Z1ADSPC' of type ADSPC_SPC in MARA table?

✍ **ANSWER**

First create the segment you require with transaction code WE31. Then you can create the material master 03 extension through transaction code WE30 Choose the radio button, Extension and create. There is a user exit for IDOC extensions. In outbound systems you have to define what should go into your extension and in the inbound system what to do with the data stored in the extension. Read or save it to your MARA table extension, but you must use an ABAP to do so.

☞ QUESTION 182

ALE Change Pointers

We plan to trigger automatic IDOCs by activating change pointers of message type HRMD_A. We will send these IDOCs by ALE to another system. If we activate the change pointers in the second system for the same message type will this automatically trigger again the changes which came in by ALE from the first system? How should we approach this?

✍ ANSWER

Consider creating some type of ownership in your two systems (a category field). You can filter outbound IDOCs by ownership. If the system is not the owner, do not create an IDOC, write an ABAP that deletes changes pointers of records that are not owned by the local system. Allowing changes to every record in both systems will cause dysfunction. Imagine one record is changed on both systems simultaneously. It is not mandatory to use MDM solve these kind of problems, but in some cases it is definitely helpful.

☞ QUESTION 183

Format Description For IDOC Invoice

I need to program an interface to output IDOC invoices for SAP. Where do I find documentation about the format?

✍ ANSWER

Ask your partner to supply the necessary documentation concerning the IDOCs that they wish to use. They can do this by downloading the description via transaction code WE60 and mailing it to you. They should supply documentation anyway because they may be using extensions (extra segments) that are specific to them. Also they will be expecting fields populated with certain values, the description of these values and where to place them should be given too.

☞ QUESTION **184**

Transport Request

This configuration did not generate a transport request. How can I move the configuration that I performed at transaction code WE20 to the QAs environment?

✍ ANSWER

Your local system name changes and you have input it again in the QA box. If you've got a distribution model you can generate transaction codes WE20 or WE21.

☞ **QUESTION 185**

Internal Unit To ISO Unit Conversion

For a specific inbound IDOC processing I receive the error " NO valid unit of measurement can be determined for ISO code CS." Is there any other way to remove this error other than creating an ISO code for CS?

✍ **ANSWER**

Create a conversion rule to map CS to the right ISO code in your system using transaction codes BD79 and BD55. There is a user exit in SAP where you can change the data of the IDOC so you can make conversion into ISO code.

☞ QUESTION **186**

Material Master & BOMMAT

I have inbound message type material master and BOMMAT and would like to send a status message to inform the sender system whether the IDOC is posted successful or not. Does SAP provide any IDOC message type for this function though? If it does, do you know how to configure it? At the moment, I only know that for Outbound IDOC, there is message type SYSTAT for sending status back to receiver system.

✍ ANSWER

Try report RDBSTATE to create ALEAUD IDOCs. These contain information about the IDOCs in your system. You need to add this IDOC type to your distribution model and partner profile.

☞ **QUESTION 187**

Storing XML File Via SAP Business Connector

Presently I am working on SAPBC. My task is to send material master IDOCs from SAP to BC. In turn BC converts IDOCs to XML (outbound in SAP and inbound for BC). Where can I store the XML file?

✍ **ANSWER**

If you are testing, you can use SAVEPIPELINETOFILE service to store the whole pipeline. Otherwise, there is a sample file service called sample.IO.utils.fileWriter:openFileWriter WritefileWriter and CloseFileWriter that can write files. You can use the pub.client:smtp service to email the file to yourself.

☞ QUESTION **188**

RBDAPP01 in Parallel

I am trying to run RBDAPP01 in parallel. The problem I have is that the program takes up all the dialog work processors. We are only using one machine so we cannot use Server Groups. What should we do?

✍ ANSWER

It needs a dialog process for every instance it is running in. You either need to run it only once, or be careful that you don't use all dialog processes. If you are in a hurry to process IDOCs manually, run three concurrently, but never more than that.

☞ QUESTION 189

Vendor Master Data Through ALE

How can I transfer vendor master data from R/3 to CRM through ALE?

✍ ANSWER

Transaction code BD14 is to send to vendor masters, but first you need to set up RFC destinations in transaction code SM59 and the ALE data distribution model in transaction code BD64.

☞ QUESTION 190

Sending Vendor Master Records

BD14 is to send vendor masters, but first you need to set up rfc destinations (SM59) and the ALE data distribution model (BD64). It is not too hard, and there are plenty of web resources to tell you how to do it.

✍ ANSWER

Yes, they need to be in int_EDIDD in the correct order. Some segments rely on other segments. For example, you couldn't have all your E1EDP01's together and then all the E1EDP19's at the bottom, because the system needs to know which E1EDP19's go with each E1EDP01.

☞ QUESTION 191

Avoiding Duplicate Postings In SAP Through EDI

When a customer sends a large file that contains many purchase order IDOCs, only a few of these IDOCs are passing through the ALE bridge. They are not posted as sales orders in SAP, and the ALE bridge is getting disconnected. Since the ALE bridge disconnects without passing the entire file to SAP, the next time it will again pass the same file into SAP. Because of this, very few of the purchase orders were duplicating in SAP (those already successfully posted in SAP first time). How do we handle this situation to avoid duplicate entries into SAP?

✍ ANSWER

Process the IDOCs immediately when sending to SAP. If you have a large number of IDOCs then this may take some time. Do not let your subsystem wait for this, since it is SAP that should handle the IDOCs. You can set your EDI customer profile to process by background instead of trigger immediately. The IDOCs will be sent to SAP only. Within SAP you can create a job that processes the IDOCs in background.

☞ QUESTION **192**

XML To IDOC Via SAP Business Connector

How do I convert the XML data to IDOC in SAP business connector

✍ ANSWER

Follow these steps. Export your IDOC structure using transaction code WE60 (menu option create DTD). Import this into BC as a record list. Create a new routing rule to your SAP system from external partner.

Create a new flow to map your XML into the IDOCs structure. At the last step in the flow, call the routing rule created from the previous step.

A typical flow:

1. Document to record to convert XML post data into pipeline record.

2. Map loop to convert xml structure.

3. Transform flat to hierarchy to convert IDOC structure into EDIDD,EDIDC data.

4. IDOC_INBOUND_ASYNCHRONOUS (or flow from step 4 above)

☞ **QUESTION 193**

Download Via the RFC_ABAP_INSTALL_ AND_RUN

I execute a program via the RFC_ABAP_INSTALL_AND_ RUN. In this program I have created a table that I would like transferred on my working station. Is there a function that will recognize my workstation for the execution of my program.

✍ **ANSWER**

RFC cannot write to your PC because it does not run in a dialog process. You need to write the file to the application server (with OPEN DATASET).

☞ QUESTION 194

BAPI For Uploading Data

I need to upload planned data to create planned independent requirements in transaction code MD61 by using BADI or BAPI. How do I do this?

✑ ANSWER

Planned independent requirements can be created using this BAPI. To do this, the item and scheduling data must be transferred. The item data is transferred back after the successful creation of a planned independent requirement. Errors that possibly occur are identified using the parameter RETURN.

☞ QUESTION 195

Stop Message Type Triggers

I am creating outbound IDOCs for sales order confirmation. Based on storage location values I have to restrict line items that should go into IDOCs. I am using program ZXVEDU02 to write the code and achieve this. When there are no line items to be sent in a sales order to a particular partner, I have to drop the IDOC itself. I want to stop the triggering of message types also. How do I do this?

✍ ANSWER

Write an output requirement on transaction BA00 output type in NACE. You must do this to perform extra checks before the output is even issued. This output requirement gets called before the IDOC processing has even started. Another option is to copy program RSNASTED to another Z version to put in extra checking logic. You then need to link your new Z program in txn NACE to the output type for EDI instead of RSNASTED. If you try to error the IDOC from within the IDOC processing function ZXVEDU02, you will not get a clean process.

☞ QUESTION 196

Outbound Processing In Batch

I have done the configuration for outbound invoice IDOCs. The receiver side is asking it to send in a BATCH, an envelope type format. For example, if there are 100 documents, they should receive a single file with 100 entries while the SAP side is sending all 100 records individually. How can I configure this?

✍ ANSWER

In your outbound partner profile, set it to collect IDOCs. Schedule job for RSEOUT00 periodically with processing mode 4. Collect IDOCs and transfer.

☞ **QUESTION 197**

AR Customer Master Creation Via IDOC

I wish to create an inbound interface that updates SAP's A/R customer master via IDOCs. I want to replicate the functionality in transactions FD01 and FD02. The message type DEBMAS looks like a good candidate, however I am receiving the following error when trying to create an IDOC using the test tool: Message no. FB121 Trans. 1 XD01: Sales org.not entered; sales area is not being processed. I don't want to create any sales data segments so I'm not sure why the Sales Org would be required.

✍ **ANSWER**

Remove the E1KNVVM with all its sub-segments. You must delete it or SAP tries to create a sales view with an empty sales area. For testing create an IDOC using transaction code BD12 and then modify (transaction code BD87 or WE05) or use it as a template (transaction code WE19).

You also have to ensure that the sender and receiver is customized to organizational structure and check the tables that it is in sync.

☞ QUESTION **198**

EDI 820 & 823

What are the SAP standard IDOC types that match EDI 820 & 823?

✍ ANSWER

The IDOC 820 is REMADV (PEXR2002) and 823 is LOCKBX (FINSTA01)

☞ QUESTION 199

Status 62 IDOC

Is there a program for processing status 62 IDOCs?

✍ ANSWER

Use program RBDCHSTA. You can get a list of all status programs by running either RBDINPUT or RBDOUTPU programs.

☞ QUESTION **200**

IDOC Deletion

How do you delete an IDOC that hasn't been successfully processed?

✍ ANSWER

You cannot delete the IDOC from the database but you can mark the IDOC for deletion, which changes the status from error 51 or 56 to error 68. Follow this pathway: Go to transaction BD87 --> highlight the IDOC you need to mark for deletion and select the option restrict and process --> it navigates you to another prog --> uncheck the import in background --> execute --> Now you can see the button mark the IDOC for deletion. Also, the programs are RBDMANI2 (for 51 status to 68) and RBDAGAI2 (for 56 to 68)

☞ QUESTION 201

Tracking Document Changes

In our sales order process, some serial numbers of the products are added manually after the order is closed. Everyday I need a download with the new added serial numbers of that day and their order number, plus order line, so I need to track the changed orders. My question is how, or in which table can I find the document changes? Maybe there are some standard reports or something?

✍ ANSWER

Use the field:OBJECTCLASS in CDHDR and CDPOS = 'VERKBELEG' for sales orders.

INDEX

Attention SAP Experts

Have you ever considered writing a book in your area of SAP? Equity Press is the leading provider of knowledge products in SAP applications consulting, development, and support. If you have a manuscript or an idea of a manuscript, we'd love to help you get it published!

Please send your manuscript or manuscript ideas to jim@sapcookbook.com – we'll help you turn your dream into a reality.

Or mail your inquiries to:

Equity Press Manuscripts
BOX 706
Riverside, California
92502

Tel (951)788-0810
Fax (951)788-0812

50% Off your next
SAPCOOKBOOK order

If you plan of placing an order for 10 or more books from www.sapcookbook.com you qualify for volume discounts. Please send an email to books@sapcookbook.com or phone 951-788-0810 to place your order.

You can also fax your orders to 951-788-0812 .

Interview books are great for cross-training

In the new global economy, the more you know the better. The sharpest consultants are doing everything they can to pick up more than one functional area of SAP. Each of the following Certification Review / Interview Question books provides an excellent starting point for your module learning and investigation. These books get you started like no other book can – by providing you the information that you really need to know, and fast.

SAPCOOKBOOK Interview Questions, Answers, and Explanations

ABAP	-	SAP ABAP Certification Review: SAP ABAP Interview Questions, Answers, and Explanations
SD	-	SAP SD Interview Questions, Answers, and Explanations
Security	-	SAP Security: SAP Security Essentials
HR	-	mySAP HR Interview Questions, Answers, and Explanations: SAP HR Certification Review
BW	-	SAP BW Ultimate Interview Questions, Answers, and Explanations: SAW BW Certification Review
	-	SAP SRM Interview Questions Answers and Explanations
Basis	-	SAP Basis Certification Questions: Basis Interview Questions, Answers, and Explanations
MM	-	SAP MM Certification and Interview Questions: SAP MM Interview Questions, Answers, and Explanations

SAP BW Ultimate Interview Questions, Answers, and Explanations

Key Topics Include:

- The most important BW settings to know
- BW tables and transaction code quick references
- Certification Examination Questions
- Extraction, Modeling and Configuration
- Transformations and Administration
- Performance Tuning, Tips & Tricks, and FAQ
- Everything a BW resource needs to know before an interview

mySAP HR Interview Questions, Answers, and Explanations

Key topics include:

- The most important HR settings to know
- mySAP HR Administration tables and transaction code quick references
- SAP HR Certification Examination Questions
- Org plan, Compensation, Year End, Wages, and Taxes
- User Management, Transport System, Patches, and Upgrades
- Benefits, Holidays, Payroll, and Infotypes
- Everything an HR resource needs to know before an interview

SAP SRM Interview Questions, Answers, and Explanations

Key Topics Include:

- The most important SRM Configuration to know
- Common EBP Implementation Scenarios
- Purchasing Document Approval Processes
- Supplier Self Registration and Self Service (SUS)
- Live Auctions and Bidding Engine, RFX Processes (LAC)
- Details for Business Intelligence and Spend Analysis
- EBP Technical and Troubleshooting Information

SAP MM Interview Questions, Answers, and Explanations

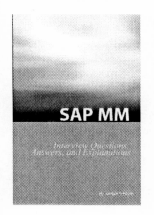

- The most important MM Configuration to know
- Common MM Implementation Scenarios
- MM Certification Exam Questions
- Consumption Based Planning
- Warehouse Management
- Material Master Creation and Planning
- Purchasing Document Inforecords

SAP SD Interview Questions, Answers, and Explanations

- The most important SD settings to know
- SAP SD administration tables and transaction code quick references
- SAP SD Certification Examination Questions
- Sales Organization and Document Flow Introduction
- Partner Procedures, Backorder Processing, Sales BOM
- Backorder Processing, Third Party Ordering, Rebates and Refunds
- Everything an SD resource needs to know before an interview

SAP Basis Interview Questions, Answers, and Explanations

- The most important Basis settings to know
- Basis Administration tables and transaction code quick references
- Certification Examination Questions
- Oracle database, UNIX, and MS Windows Technical Information
- User Management, Transport System, Patches, and Upgrades
- Backup and Restore, Archiving, Disaster Recover, and Security
- Everything a Basis resource needs to know before an interview

SAP Security Essentials

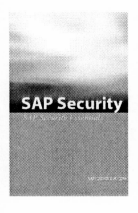

- Finding Audit Critical Combinations
- Authentication, Transaction Logging, and Passwords
- Roles, Profiles, and User Management
- ITAR, DCAA, DCMA, and Audit Requirements
- The most important security settings to know
- Security Tuning, Tips & Tricks, and FAQ
- Transaction code list and table name references

SAP Workflow Interview Questions, Answers, and Explanations

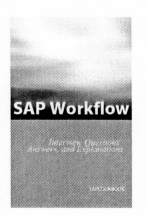

- Database Updates and Changing the Standard
- List Processing, Internal Tables, and ALV Grid Control
- Dialog Programming, ABAP Objects
- Data Transfer, Basis Administration
- ABAP Development reference updated for 2006!
- Everything an ABAP resource needs to know before an interview

Printed in the United Kingdom
by Lightning Source UK Ltd.
119088UK00001B/62